THINKING IN THE FUTURE TENSE

Edward B. Lindaman

Thinking in the Future Tense

Broadman Press
Nashville, Tennessee

Dewey Decimal Classification: 301.24
Subject Heading: FUTURISM
Library of Congress Catalog Card Number: 77–91270
Printed in the United States of America

Preface

One of the most delightful and important miracles of life occurs in the subtle merging of the person "I am now" with the "person not yet." This is the miracle of being stretched—stretched to being "more than I am."

Sometimes the causative forces are within: A burst of inexplicable courage that propels us beyond real or imagined barriers, a sudden surge of energy, a bold idea, a spontaneous decision to act, the welling up and overflowing of faith and hope and love. Usually we surprise even ourselves at these moments.

Sometimes the forces are exterior: Someone, maybe a friend or a mentor, forces us to dig deeper than we ever would have on our own and helps us discover resources we never dreamed we had. Or it may be a cataclysmic event—a death that shakes us to our boots, a traumatic loss, a disaster that tumbles down walls and reveals new avenues and possibilities. Other times it is something simple that turns the trick—a word or an embrace, a gorgeous sunset, a phrase that speaks directly and healingly to a deep need. More often, it is a combination of people, events, and happenings that bumps us out of a rut and sets us on a swift new course.

For me, the stretching miracles have often occurred in grappling with books—books that transported me into realms I either did not yet understand or which were far richer than I had imagined. These intellectual encounters have a way of becoming emotional and spiritual encounters as well; a truth enters my consciousness and, like new blood flowing through a tube into a vein, it quickly permeates every fiber of my being, imperceptibly but irreversibly changing who I am.

In preparing this book, I have drawn upon the genius of many different writers from a wide variety of professions, with the hope that this synthesis might help trigger other "stretching miracles." I have given credit to those authors from whom I have knowingly borrowed, but in many cases the germ of one writer's words has blended so completely with other ideas that I have lost track of where I first encountered them.

In addition to presenting fragments of ideas from some of the most brilliant thinkers of our time, this book reflects who I am—where I have been and where I am going. It has been tempered by my vocational roles in the aerospace, aircraft, and electronics industries; by experience in industrial management and educational administration; by avocational involvement in the life of local and national YMCA and the Church; by being a husband and parent of four children; and by wide exposure to people all across the nation whom I have had the privilege of knowing in connection with lectures I have given and seminars I have led. Scores of people have unknowingly contributed their ideas to this book—to each one, recognized or not, I am deeply grateful. Yet I assume full responsibility for this synthesis and expression.

This is not a novel or a publication that can be picked up and read at one sitting and then discarded. Rather, it is intended as a "workbook." It is something to tackle in pieces. Some parts are more complex than others; some fit cleanly with the rest and others may seem disconnected.

I trust no one will swallow all of it; the contents are a collection of ideas that I have found to be powerful images for going beyond what I thought to be possible. Some ideas you may disagree with, or find irrelevant to your life. Some ideas will evoke strong feelings—positive or negative, or both. Some ideas may seem obscure or flimsy, and others powerful and timely. But however you react, I recommend that you struggle more than just a little with the portions that at first reading seem "too far out" or non-sense.

My own experience is that if I understand 25 percent of a book the first time through, I have locked onto something worth reading again and again. Paul Tillich's *The New Being* was like that for me. Over the period of several years, I have finally begun to grasp what he was saying, but I had to keep at it.

This is not a book of predictions about the future. Rather, I believe you will find this to be a compendium of provocative possibilities and unsettling questions. The book introduces some of the most powerful ideas of our time. The contents are not topics that most of us dwell upon daily, but they represent the landscape of what we *should* begin to claim as familiar territory.

This is a landscape embracing science, technology, education, religion; it is diverse and yet characterized by wholeness. The future we are talking about is not the future of medicine, the future of space, art, recreation, or even the future of my life or your life. The future is global: the future of humanity. But, amazingly, the global future is rooted in the private, personal futures of individuals. This paradox, both inspiring and humbling, is discussed from a variety of perspectives throughout the book.

This is not yet another futuristic vision of a coming utopia or a coming end of the world. I have deliberately not painted a picture of the future. *This is up to you to do for yourself.* That is the whole point: Each of us can consciously imagine, think about, project, hope for, dream about, plan for the future. The thrust of this book is to help you paint your own future without being limited to the ideas of others.

One thread that runs through the book is the image of our time in history as a time "between." I find that no matter what I am doing or wherever I am, if I hear the sound of a train whistle off in the distance, I immediately think of my youth. Maybe it is because I grew up in a small Midwestern town, and a train came through twice a day and always whistled at the crossings in and out of town. That sound evokes vivid images of my past; it never fails. On the other hand, whenever I encounter an infant—whether in an airline terminal, a grocery store, or when my two-year-old granddaughter comes to visit— I invariably think about the future and what that child's children might experience.

These are the two poles of life—past and future. Each of us has different symbols which hitch us to the past and the future, and yet we live in the present. Regrettably, most of our consciousness is dotted with representations of the past; we have been oriented to the past. But now that we have the technical skills to invent a completely new world, we must increasingly, and quickly, become more oriented to the future. Quite simply, we must learn how to "think in the future tense."

I hope these few chapters help in that crucial turning around. What a tremendous opportunity we have. With William Irwin Thompson, author of the profound book, *Evil and World Order,* I submit that we are in the beginning stages of a new renaissance at least as sweeping and revolutionary as "The Renaissance" five centuries ago.

Thompson believes this new renaissance is fueled by the *coming together* of two opposite character types—the "mystic" and the "systems engineer." Those of the "mystic" type are comfortable with the mystery of things, they acknowledge the unknowns, and they are inner-oriented, accepting, and deeply trusting of feelings and intuition. Those of the "systems-engineer" type are most comfortable with tasks and facts; merely give them a job to do and they do it; give them a problem and they find a solution.

But now, writes Thompson, we find the two realms working in conjunction as well as opposition. In their connecting and colliding we have moved to a new kind of expression: with new vision, new energies, new breakthroughs. Objectivity merges with subjectivity and a new consciousness is born.

I find this tremendously fascinating and challenging. Just as no one "managed" the Renaissance of the fifteenth century, no one is managing this one. But this time we have a general awareness of the changes and our potential in guiding them. We have the awesome dual responsibility of being *able to* construct our own future and having to choose *whether to* and *how to* participate in that creative process; then we have to *decide what options* we prefer.

The point is that the bases for the images that pull us into the future ought to be our own, chosen freely, the fruits of our creativity and unique perspective rather than someone else's prescriptions for tomorrow.

If this book encourages or activates your creative urge, your willingness to assume responsibility for the future, and if it strikes a chord of community, shared dreams, and commitment, we all shall be the richer.

Edward B. Lindaman
Whitworth College
Spokane, Washington

Contents

Contents

He who fights the future fights a dangerous enemy. The future is not. It borrows its strength from the man himself and when it has tricked him out of this it stands outside him as the enemy he must meet.

Kierkegaard

Throughout our lives we walk with a ghostly multitude, companions from all our pasts, faces known and unknown, those who went before us and made us humanly possible, the commensals of our cultural selves. Their impatience is our legacy from them; and it animates our feet and eyes. In their lore, in their letters, in treasured memories of their words, and perhaps in other less understood ways, they are always there, seemingly our "familiars." But, while they may have guided us to the antechamber of our longings, they can only freeze at the door. We respond to the dreams they dreamed before us. We look backward in order to follow the direction of their pointing fingers. But in the lurch of our encounter with our Castle vision **they all leave us.** *The Castle is of the living; and we can perceive it only at living moments.*[1]

Malachi Martin

The crises of our times are not only signs of decay. They are also signs of expectant birth. We live in the Between Times, the time of decision. It is a time of transition from the death of the old civilization to the emergence of the new. We are not sure of what the new will be, but we know and feel the reality of its growing existence within us.[2]

Gerald and Patricia Mische

13

1
Thinking in the Future Tense

It used to be that the future, like the weather, was something that everyone talked about but that remained totally beyond human control. Now all of that has changed. Today we not only dream about the future, worry over it, save for it, and invest in it; we also are consciously and unconsciously creating our future. Goal-setting has been institutionalized. The "power of positive thinking" energizes championship teams, supersalesmen, dieters, and aspiring artists.

And yet, even as we begin to flex these newly discovered "muscles," we are somewhat confused about the idea of dealing with the future. We assume, as a general rule, that the "future" is tomorrow—when in fact the short-range is but a fraction of legitimate concern. Similarly, we regard the future as a subject of quite limited scope; I think of *my* company's profit potential, *my* family's summer vacation, *my* career prospects. Much less frequently do we seriously consider the regional or national future, or for that matter the future of our city's schools or health-care facilities.

We err also in basing most of our assumptions about the future on the premise that what will happen someday will be much like what happens today—mostly the same, just bigger, faster, more or less of it. However, in recent years the lessons of the energy crunch, irreversible environmental damage, and innovative space technology have begun to make the point: The future may be very different

15

from today. *The future will be what we make of it.* What a revolutionary idea!

What Kind of World?

John McHale, writing eloquently in *The Future of the Future,* notes that, "The question is no longer, Can we change the world, the question now is: What kind of world do we want?" [3]

To be sure, we have barely begun to grasp this responsibility intellectually or respond with individual or corporate activity. Few of us see the whole picture; reality is the workday, weekends, some hobbies, various irritations, and smatterings of national and world news seen on television. We are far too busy to think in global terms; yet technological advances have suddenly transported us into the universe.

Thinking in the future tense is no longer a sideshow circus joke having to do with fortune-tellers and crystal balls. As stated in the recently published document of the World Future Society, *An Introduction to the Study of the Future:* "What was once regarded as a peculiar gift of the prophet or the special talent of the science-fiction writer—the ability to describe the future—is now increasingly seen as a needed, legitimate, and exciting field of intellectual endeavor."

Space Exploration

If we chose to ignore the philosophical arguments on the subject of the future, we still would be confronted by the astounding events of the new era of space exploration. Nothing so dramatically illustrates the rich potential and the awesome challenges of deciding what to do with our future as the achievements beyond earth's atmosphere since that historic day in October 1957, when Russia orbited the first man-made satellite. Our mental picture of reality—past and future—has been radically transformed.

We may laugh at the idea of earlier generations thinking that the earth was flat and that the sun was not the center of outer space. But we really do not know how to respond when we are told that new technology has suddenly enlarged several times over our knowledge of our galaxy's size. Our universe, known to scientists in 1963 to be at least four billion light years across, was measured just three years later with improved equipment and found to be about eight billion light years from one end to the other. Now our strongest telescopes have allowed scientists to photograph radio sources some 42 sextillion miles out in space. Just sixty years ago we thought that the Milky Way contained all the objects in the sky and that our sun occupied a nearly central position in it.

We have since learned that the Milky Way, a vast pinwheel of some 100 billion stars, is rotating and is actually about 100,000 light years from end to end and 15,000 light years thick. Our solar system, off to one side of the galaxy, moves across it every 200 million years. And in 1977, we learned that our galaxy is streaking through the universe at a velocity greater than one million miles per hour, heading away from the constellation Aquarius and toward the constellation Leo.

A second galaxy, the Great Andromeda, has been discovered. It is some 2.2 million light years distant. The Andromeda and the Milky Way form a part of a cluster of about twenty galaxies known as the "Local Group." (In all, tens of billions of galaxies, each thousands of light years in diameter and separated from other galaxies by much greater reaches of space, are thought to exist.)

Perhaps the most startling of all the new findings in recent years came late in 1977, just a few months after NASA launched its largest-yet unmanned satellite—a high-energy astronomy observatory (HEAO-1). For many years scientists have believed that the dominant component of the universe was contained in the dense masses of the billions of stars. But according to early HEAO-1 measurements, the principal component is contained in what we formerly thought of as the "emptiness" of space. But space is not empty at all; it consists of a thin spread of gases, mainly oxygen. Amazingly, the combined mass of this "wisp" of gases would, if constant throughout space, far exceed the combined mass of all the stars. Says Richard C. Henry, deputy director of NASA's astrophysics program, "If this proves correct, it will mean HEAO-1 has really just discovered the universe."

The universe, we now know, is expanding; the galaxies are flying apart at barely imaginable speeds. The old picture of a static universe is gone. We can monitor the birth and death of stars. Clouds of gas and dust and entire galaxies are formed and dispersed. The heavens, alive with motion and change, are even yet an immense mystery.

We are just beginning to discover how blind and deaf we have been. Our world and the supposed emptiness of interstellar space are drenched with color, sound, and waves that our limited human eyes and ears do not perceive without aid. Our human organs are tuned to only a few octaves in a scale that stretches out prodigiously in both directions, from microwaves through cosmic waves on to waves that are a mile in length.

Knowledge Augmented

Our growing knowledge of "beyond earth" was augmented by space probes and the more spectacular manned lunar landings of this decade. Following the mesmerizing landing on the moon by three American astronauts in 1969, scientists dared to dream of other steps in space exploration. One of the most logical steps was a manned landing on Mars that would have cost upwards of 100 billion dollars. But public support for such a costly venture was non-existent, and the idea was shelved. National Aeronautics and Space Administration planners also talked about modifying a distant planet to make it habitable. One report explored colonizing Mars, using new kinds of plants in order to develop some form of agriculture in that harsh environment. It was thought this might involve "cell reassembly." Another highly speculative proposal was to attempt to make Venus habitable. This plan would involve seeding the planet's upper atmosphere with an organism that utilizes carbon dioxide and produces oxygen. This zone of organisms would gradually float to the planet's surface, it was reasoned, thereby reducing its temperature as the carbon dioxide content was reduced.

Government officials and NASA planners, alert to public opinion, determined that a more modest program could be financed. Accordingly, we began building and launching relatively small instrumented probes to nearby planets and into other parts of the solar system—and beyond. These are the *Viking, Pioneer, Voyager,* and *Mariner* spacecraft.

The decision regarding manned space exploration moved from planetary to near-earth programs with the notion of first creating a very low-cost "shuttle service" back and forth from the surface of the earth to orbits a couple of hundred miles out. This twenty-first-century "clipper ship" would virtually unlock the door to economically feasible space exploration and habitation.*

* The proper context of this development is historical. The wheel enabled mankind to traverse land with loads of possessions. It changed our ability to function and to explore. Invention of the boat likewise enabled us to go new places and dramatically changed the parameters of existence. Then, early in this century, a third method of transportation—the airplane—further expanded man's ability to move about the globe. Each of these three new capabilities revolutionized our ability to function. We are now witnessing the fourth! The space shuttle gives us the ability to colonize near-earth space.

For example, if we ultimately do decide to go to Mars, the place to build the spaceship for it is in orbit; and the place from which to launch it is in orbit, *not* from the surface of earth. That is why the space shuttle, *Enterprise,* is the keystone to many different future space activities.

With access to near-earth space, a myriad of new possibilities come into being. Early in the 1980's, for example, a space telescope using the shuttle will be launched. An optical 10-inch telescope above the atmosphere is equal to a 100-inch telescope on the ground. Very soon such a telescope, roughly 90 inches in diameter, will increase the volume of space we can comprehend by 250 times. Stars seven times dimmer than those we can now see will become observable. We will find out, as one of the very first technical outputs of that project, whether or not there are planetary systems around other stars. And if so, the probability of extraterrestrial life increases by orders of magnitude. We will soon have a lot more to think about! *

The space shuttle also will make it possible and affordable to launch and maintain sophisticated international communication satellites. We can have very large antennas in space and very small transmitters on the ground. Instead of having just a few places around the world that can communicate via satellites, every home and every individual will be able to talk to other individuals through a satellite with an antenna no larger than can be carried in a wrist-

---

* Since Galileo, astronomers have been giving mankind one after another new realities to ponder and eventually place in the context of all that we *thought* we had known. Surely one of the most intriguing such findings in this decade is evidence of what astronomers have labeled "black holes"—stars that have collapsed into such tremendously dense states and possess such high gravitational fields that even light cannot escape. NASA's new high-energy astronomy observatory has begun to study via X rays one such black hole, dubbed Circinus X-1. Early results seem to confirm the existence of these powerful lightless stars.

watch. These capabilities will radically restructure the whole telecommunications industry. And we should be alert to the second- and third-order social consequences of such technology; careful and exhaustive thinking in the future tense is required.

As access to near-earth space becomes more economical, satellite surveillance of the surface of the earth will expand tremendously. Two *Landsat* satellites currently do this by continuously taking color photographs of the surface of the earth in several different spectra and, through a television link, send the data back to earth for analysis. The ability to observe, monitor, and measure agricultural and geological resources opens up new levels of stewardship. Thus far, information from *Landsat* has been available to anyone wanting it, regardless of country. As the United States continues to provide repetitive global multispectral data to all users, opportunities for international cooperation will be advanced.

Further Advances

Gathering data about the weather—climatic research—is still another application of our new technology. To better understand how and why the climate is changing, our scientists are planning spacecraft to measure and collect such sophisticated data as global absorption and reflection of solar energy, sea surface temperatures, worldwide soil moisture content, solar radiation absorption and reflection, and stratospheric ozone levels.

Repetitive access to space also opens the way to a new kind of industrialization. The qualities of outer space—vacuum, sterility, low temperature, and zero gravity—provide a ready-made environment for a number of vital industrial activities such as materials processing and manufacture of chemical and physical products.

The space shuttle may mean new energy sources, too.

Technology now exists for building a space station that would generate electrical power from the sun. A nonpolluting, environmentally acceptable, virtually inexhaustible energy source is within our grasp. NASA scientists feel it might take half a generation to test a solar-powered space station in the full systems context of operational, routine, reliable energy delivery.

As indicated in this brief outline of possibles, in the next few years our government and scientists will be making a number of major policy decisions in the area of space applications. But the choice of whether or not to exploit this new energy source via a solar generating station is probably the most significant one of all.

The World of 2000

Thinking ahead just twenty-two years, it is easy to see that on New Year's Eve, 1999, as you list your resolutions for the year 2000, your world will be so utterly different that any attempt to describe it would be futile. But we might look at just one of the ways in which change may come—cooperation.

Cooperation

The possibilities of cooperation that modern technological society offers are staggering, especially in a historical perspective. Human beings are aggressive, yes, and also cooperative. For example, shortly before the year 3000 B.C., cooperative efforts (not necessarily voluntary) raised the great pyramids. But the intricacy of detail in planning, communicating, and transport in pyramid building is negligible compared to the cooperation required today for airing a single network television program when we consider all that is involved in bringing together personnel, equipment, design, manufacture, selling, transportation, and administration.

The cooperative effort behind a single TV broadcast is infinitesimal compared to the *Apollo* flights to the moon and back when 400,000 persons in 20,000 companies in every state in the union, over a period of about six years, built fifteen million parts that functioned together perfectly!

Massive cooperation is the hallmark of a technological society. Not one of us can disengage from the cooperative network of modern living. To be aware of the need for cooperation and the fact of our demonstrated ability to cooperate links us to a hopeful tomorrow.

Key Questions

Learning to think in the future tense will demand of us consideration of hundreds of ideas not yet pondered. But already we know some of the key questions we must consider.

One of these has to do with *technology assessment*. In 1962 Alan T. Waterman, then the director of the United States National Science Foundation, stated: "Science, in its pure form, is not concerned with where discoveries may lead; its disciples are interested in discovering the truth." While some scientists still hold this view, others are insisting that science more intentionally pursue social goals and that this be in cooperation with social and political sectors. Few people outside the scientific community realize what extraordinary progress has been made in the last quarter-century under this regime of uncircumscribed exploration. The unlocking of the molecular basis for biology was the beginning of an entirely new understanding of the life processes. The discovery of the atomic basis led to completely new understandings of the structure and behavior of inanimate matter. Dramatic discoveries were made in cosmology, earth sciences, high-energy physics, and astronomy.

In June 1976 a small group of well-known international scientists met in Bellagio, Italy. Speaking for the conference, Lewis M. Branscomb of International Business Machines said, "The success with which human affairs are managed will (therefore) depend strongly on the involvement of scientists and engineers with social and political institutions that determine the use of technology. We believe that the readiness, indeed the eagerness, of most scientists and engineers to meet this obligation is a basis of optimism for the future prospects for humanity."

Two and one-half years earlier, Public Law 92–484 created a special research arm of the Congress called the "Office of Technology Assessment" (OTA). Since that time OTA has been asked by Congress to undertake assessments in a wide variety of areas, including energy, the oceans, health, materials resources, food, transportation, technology, and world trade. OTA's basic purpose is to assist Congress in anticipating and planning for the consequences of technological change. Its task is to examine the many ways, both expected and uncertain, in which technology might affect people's lives *before* decisions are made.

With federal research and development expenditures reaching upwards of 25 billion dollars annually, a technology-assessment function becomes virtually indispensable to thinking in the future tense.

Social Indicators

Another arena of decision making is *social indicators.* Without question, we presently have extremely poor methods of measuring societal trends, other than economic. Coming upon us rapidly between now and the year 2000 will be the development of social indicators whereby we can monitor American life as to quality, direction, and rate of change. Are we getting healthier? Is pollution increasing? What causes voting registration and balloting to fluctuate? Do children learn more than they used to? How many people are really alienated? What constitutes an adequate housing situation? What constitutes poverty?

Needed during the rest of this century will be more concrete and valid judgments about the true condition of American society. Snap judgments based upon fragmentary television or newspaper accounts will no longer suffice. We need to accurately relate expenditures, effort, and concern on a priority basis. Social indices will constitute the feedback system that allows us to tie finally programs to results.

Decisions become more and more complicated as technology cuts across legal, organizational, procedural, and managerial systems, as they make geographical and political boundaries meaningless. When we ponder the *macrotechnological era* just ahead—replete with satellites monitoring weather, crops, forest fires, tidal waves, and pollution, with vacuum welding and freeze-drying foods in outer space, with reflective discs providing nighttime illumination and solar energy—we are considering more than simply new capabilities. Each new capability has incredible multinational ramifications. We are entering a complicated round of new value generation that will affect the lives of peasant and politician alike. Nothing less than innovative involvement and action in diplomatic, political, national, and international systems will suffice.

Educational Change

Education, too, is a major arena of change. By the year 2000 we may expect between 60 to 70 percent of our college-age youth (15 million) to be in college. Can we safely detain millions of active American youth simply by building more and bigger universities? I doubt it. Something quite drastic will have to take place, for the alteration of the scale of education will bring problems that doubling and redoubling of conventional resources will never answer. I cannot predict exactly what form this new direction in education will take, but I do know that the role of smaller, independent institutions will probably increase, due to their superiority in personalizing learning experiences. The inherent flexibility of small-college administrations and faculties allows quick institutional responses to new opportunities. Small colleges will excell in innovative practices—not in graduate work, the specialty of the major university, and not in vocational training, the province of the community college, but in the four-year undergraduate college education emphasizing the liberal arts.

Among the factors that will drive higher education into new directions are the sheer economics of college administration, new discoveries in learning theory, and the recognition (finally) of the rate of obsolescence of knowledge. (We now know that "intellectual capital" can be rapidly used up. There was a time when we could attend college for four or six years and, in effect, store up a reasonable amount of "capital" to last for many years. This is no longer the case. It is quite possible that we will soon see a "self-destruct" diploma: a diploma that will be invalid five or ten years after it is issued *unless* some proof of continued learning is offered! Guided independent study and lifelong learning will become more and more attractive.

Education will be more highly goal-oriented. One goal might be to view ourselves as "users" instead of consumers. Another might be to develop a sense of critical intelligence so that we will not be overly manipulated. Or we might strive to learn how to work with people who are different, or to develop an openness that permits contemplation of all plans for human betterment.

These four arenas—technology assessment, social indicators, macrotechnology, and education—illustrate the complexity and potential of some of the most vital futures thinking just ahead. We are mere infants toying with global powers: conscious assessment of the things we make and do before we make or implement them; objectively measuring all manner of societal and global behavior and factoring precise interpretations out of massive accumulations of data; organizing multinational systems to handle information from "space colonies" providing such services as global resource monitoring, global communications, and global energy production and transmission; and goal-oriented educational systems which promote self-responsibility on the part of learners.

Our Own Significance

No one has, as yet, adequately named this age. We must leave that for the philosophers and historians, but after centuries of maturation the hour has come when we are seeing our own significance in the physical world. We are struggling to master the overwhelming dimensions of the universe and at the very same time studying the infinitesimal with electron microscopes that magnify 150,000 times. One after another, all fields of human endeavor are being shaken.

Too often we refer to the *re* of things. We pine for the golden age of the past. We want to re-create yesterday, re-store something we have, re-turn to simple times. In fact we cannot go back. A person never returns to a childhood, and a corporation never returns to a single owner. Our vision needs to be for the *new creation.*

Today we look out of our suburban dens (which have replaced our prehistoric caves), and we blink our eyes with the sudden realization that, thanks to science, all the filters have been removed from between us and everything that happens anywhere in the world. *Responsibility has been handed back to us as individuals.*

Standing at the threshold between the age of gravity and the infinity of space, we must now begin to evaluate our celestial purposes. To handle this new level of responsibility we can borrow from the growing school of futurists a variety of techniques and postures which equip us to think and act wisely and with dispatch. A raft of books, readily available at the local library and bookstore, introduces us to the "shape" of the future. The most popular and well-known of these publications was Alvin Toffler's *Future Shock.* There have been many other excellent books since: *The Next 10,000 Years, The Next 500 Years, The World that Could Be, Limits to Growth, Mankind at the Turning Point, Small Is Beautiful, An Alternative for America II, An Incomplete Guide to the Future, The Survival of the Wisest,* and many, many others.

Perhaps the place to begin is in taking charge of one's own life and assuming responsibility for creating one's own future. The famous Spanish essayist José Ortega y Gasset wrote in *Man and Crisis* that people can handle almost anything life hands them *except* not being clear in one's own mind concerning what he believes about things.

Something is a problem to me not because I am ignorant about it, not because I have failed to fulfill my intellectual duties with regard to it; but when I search within myself and do not know what my genuine attitude toward it is, when among my thoughts about it I do not know which is truly mine, the one which I really believe, the one which is in full accord with me. And vice versa; *solution of a problem* does not necessarily mean the discovery of a scientific law, but only being clear with myself about the thing that was a problem to me, suddenly finding, among many ideas about it, one which I recognize as my actual and authentic attitude toward it. The

> essential, basic problem, and in this sense the only prob-
> lem, is to fit myself in with myself, to be in agreement
> with myself, to find myself.[4]

This phenomenon is especially applicable to our belief about the future. At the root of our behavior—influencing whether we look ahead timidly, poised on tiptoe and ready to retreat at the slightest upset, or whether our approach is bold and enthusiastic, seeing in challenges opportunities for growth and finding in ambiguity stimulus for new questions and new answers—is our basic position on this question: Am I really able to participate in creating my own future? Many answer that we cannot take command of the ship of life, that it is too late, and too many forces are beyond our control. These people concede the future to those who, regardless of station, wealth, or status, answer in the affirmative.

Obviously, I argue for the latter posture. The reason is quite simple. What we imagine of the future determines what it will be. Frederick Polak's exceptional book on the power of the *Image of the Future* persuasively explains how we are pulled out of the present by our image of the future. The nature of life is that we live in the present tense but we "live toward the future, and are aimed toward it." [5]

Contemplating Preferred Options

We cannot act in the future tense—we can only contemplate. And because the future is unknown, we are forced to contemplate a universe of alternatives. But here is the critical point: We contemplate not only *possible* options but also *preferred* options. This involves deciding, choosing. And once we cross this magic-like barrier something dramatic happens. We are instantly transported back to the world of the present tense where we must consider the impact of our day-to-day actions on that future. Hence, in a tremendously real sense, the future is always *now*. And to deal responsibly with the present requires contemplating the future and deciding in which directions we would prefer to move.* This is freedom in its most fundamental dimension.

The act of choosing a preferred future also implies a future step: commitment. The opposite of surrender, commitment is giving power to the direction in which one decides to move. According to Ortega, modern culture is indebted to Christendom for learning the virtue of commitment:

> If there had been no Christianity, it never would have occurred to this man to dedicate his life to anything. This is the fundamental thing in man's Christian life: to discover that life, in the final analysis, consists in having to be dedicated to something, not in busying oneself with this, that, or the other—which would be just the opposite, to put into life something which would be considered valuable—but in picking up one's entire life and surrendering it to something, dedicating it . . . this is

---

* Ironically, as this book goes to press, the American space effort would greatly benefit from such responsible and forward-looking consideration. At issue is not so much the sticky question of how much federal monies NASA should have to continue the first phases of our space-shuttle program. We certainly owe it to ourselves to adequately fund outer space exploration, but even more critical is the question of how we utilize outer space and space technology. The ideals and letter of the law of the 1958 Space Act clearly state our purpose is "to study and explore space for peaceful purposes." The fine print does acknowledge the potential military aspects of outer space, but our whole objective from the beginning was for peaceful purposes. In recent years, however, NASA has become more and more entangled in Pentagon-pushed applications entirely military in nature and intent. Americans generally are barely aware of this, but the ramifications of our nation's decisions on the use of outer and near space are extremely important—not only to generations of men and women and children around the globe. Yes, here is a place for considering not only possible options but also *preferred options*.

Christianity's basic discovery, the thing which put it indelibly into history, which is to say, into man.

Ancient man was ignorant of this; for him the good life consisted at best of bearing the blows of fortune with dignity. At its finest this was Stoicism—life as a process of enduring, Seneca's *sustine*. But since Christianity came into being, man, however aetheistic, knows and sees not only that human life ought to be the surrender of itself—that life takes on the sense of a premeditated mission and an interior density, the complete opposite of enduring an external destiny—but that whether we like it or not, life *is* this surrender. Tell me what else the phrase means which is so often repeated in the New Testament and is, like almost all the New Testament, so paradoxical: "He who loses his life shall gain it." That is to say, give your life, hand it over, surrender it; then it is truly yours, you have won it, you have saved it.

And this concept of life as the dedication of one's self to something, as a mission and not simply a discreet use of something, which has been given to us, and given already made, has its opposite side; that life is then, in its own essence, responsibility for itself.[6]

One might gain the impression that contemplating the future and committing one's self to priorities is terribly lonely and private. I think our experience in focusing on the future, even though it may be limited, makes a clear case for the benefits of shared decision-making. We decide best when we are in community with others of a like purpose. The dynamics of a community of concerned people gives power to the shared image of the future.

The advantages of community are legion. Most noteworthy, and sometimes the most anxiety producing, is the impact of diversity. Nearly every group of people which gathers together because of a shared goal, whether for negative (something the group dislikes and wants to do away with) or positive reasons (something they would like to see happen), includes some who think differently, challenge sacred assumptions, and force the group to move beyond the familiar into new territories of thought and action. Diversity within community often has the effect of keeping us from the dangers of what Geoffrey Vickers has described as "mantraps."

> Lobster pots are designed to catch lobsters. A man entering a man-sized lobster pot would become suspicious of the narrowing tunnel, he would shrink from the drop at the end; and if he fell in, he would recognize the entrance as a possible exit and climb out again—even if he were the shape of a lobster.

> A trap is a trap only for creatures which cannot solve the problems that it sets. Man-traps are dangerous only in relation to the limitations on what men can see and value and do. *The nature of the trap is a function of the nature of the trapped.* To describe either is to imply the other.

> I start with the trap, because it is more consciously familiar; we the trapped tend to take our own state of mind for granted—which is partly why we are trapped. With the shape of the trap in our minds, we shall be better able to see the relevance of our limitations and to question those assumptions about ourselves which are most inept to the activity and the experience of being human now.[7]

Tension

Diversity also tends to inject a desirable quality of tension into the realm of the present-becoming-future. Tension means that we are working on something; it is the opposite of adjustment. (I don't want to adjust to the smog of Los Angeles, I want to get rid of it.) To be tense about a concern is to acknowledge that there is a problem worth solving, a problem worth dedicating time and energy to. The tendency in the cafeteria culture of our age (refusing the portions that create unpleasantness of any sort and "buying into" only those portions that give immediate pleasures) is to avoid tension. But in tension is problem-solving. Dealing with tenseness is to seek out the causes of what is wrong with our society from the perspective of the larger good.

Indeed, it is healthy to ask what life is all about—not just for me, but for our neighbors and even those unseen millions across the globe. Thinking in the future tense necessarily relates self to the world. Unfortunately, however, the picture of our world is not very pretty; the poverty-stricken starving hardly inspire confidence in the future. It is sometimes difficult to maintain the poise of our personal hope for the future in the face of all the tragedy around us. We may be helped by viewing our situation as akin to the birth process:

> The birth image is apt. The healthy delivery of our shared future is not automatic. Nor will it be without pain. New birth seldom comes without pain. The greater the life reality seeking to be born, the greater the pain that may accompany the birth process.
>
> In the birth process, if the birth passage remains rigid and does not widen, the pain intensifies. The unborn life is in peril and the mother's life is endangered.
>
> This birth image provides insights into the pain being experienced in the human community of today. Existing socio-political structures are too rigid and narrow to give healthy delivery to new stages of human growth and development struggling to be born.
>
> But more than human development is at stake. The constriction threatens our very survival.
>
> Our task now is not to fight against our pains and crises, reacting against the symptoms—and in so doing

making present structures more rigid than before. It is rather to recognize the positive pregnancy of our times, to work with the birth spasms, giving our energies to a widening of the birth passage, *making ready the way for the birth of a new stage in human development.*[8]

Purpose Grandiose and Simple

So our purpose can be a mixture of the grandiose and the simple. We can simultaneously work to create a more just and human world order and to keep self from being lost in the storms of hatred, distrust, agony, and human need raging all around us. As Dag Hammarskjöld counseled, we are "to exist for the future of others without being suffocated by their present." I have found this to be excellent advice. Daily we are in positions where we could let another person's demands, actions, or attitudes suffocate our ability to deal with our shared future. Our role right now as human beings on planet earth is to exist for the future of others without being suffocated by their present. This will demand of us a new ability to "think in the future tense."

The fact is that the mad rush of the last 100 years has left us out of breath. We have had no time to swallow our spittle. We know that the automated machine is here to liberate us and show us the way back to Eden; that it will do for us what no revolution, no doctrine, no prayer, and no promise could do. But we do not know that we have arrived. We stand there panting, caked with sweat and dust afraid to realize that the seventh day of the second creation is here, and the ultimate sabbath is spread out before us. . . .[1]

Eric Hoffer

2
The Future Is Now

In his book, *Learning for Tomorrow,* Alvin Toffler tells
us about a tribe of natives who lived in an Amazon jungle
totally unrelated to the rest of civilization. In this tribe,
the parents, like those everywhere, were seeking to prepare
their children to live in the future. Though the process
is not necessarily an intentional one, they did base the
education of their children upon *what is* and *what has been.*
Their traditions made it clear that they had always lived
on the river. Their customs and abilities were linked to
a river culture. That was the way it was, and that obviously
continued. So they proceeded, with little question, to prepare their children for the future based upon what had
been and what then was.

However, unknown to them, up the stream a few hundred miles another tribe had developed a new technology
that enabled them to build dams. And this other tribe was
busily engaged in building a dam that would eventually
divert the headwaters of the river that supplied the liveli-
hood for the first tribe.

Preparation for the Future

I suggest that is directly analogous to the situation of
modern-day civilization. Preparation for the future is almost totally based upon what has been and what is, and
very little consideration is given to *what may be.* Our education systems have not encouraged such thinking, and like

37

the tribe in Toffler's story, we pay the penalty in all manner of human suffering.

Though the past does play an exceedingly important part in determining, and of course preparing for, our future, we need to take care that we do not merely extrapolate our future from the past. In *The Next 500 Years,* thirty-one trends are listed which have been going on for a thousand years. Urbanization, increased availability of education, humanitarianism on increase, industrialization, professionalism, rise of meritocracy, and the like are examples of trends that, at first glance, seem timeless. Admittedly, that is one way to look at the future. But the object in that case is not the future but the "future of the past."

Our Preferred Future

In *The Future of the Future,* John McHale suggests a different approach to the future. He encourages us to decide on our preferred future: to imagine what we *want*—then from that reference point work backwards toward the present, and to move toward the future of the future we envision!

The word "future" is derived from the Latin word *futura.* The future of an acorn is an oak. Given time and the right circumstances, we can predict the outcome of the future. There are many things in our society that can be looked at in that way. The future is destined almost directly by the present. However, there is another way of looking at the future. The Latin word *adventus* gives us the word "adventure." We need to see the future as adventurous and utterly open—an *adventus* future has unlimited possibilities. It is not mere extrapolation.

How easy it is to erect elaborate plans on flimsy, outdated assumptions. We all do it, and we never cease being surprised that we failed to see much earlier how things really would turn out.

You may have heard the story about the desperate fellow who because he could not take the way things were going for him jumped off the tallest skyscraper in town. Reportedly, he was heard to say as he sizzled past the second story, "I'm OK so far."

On the one hand, his comment describes the *absurd speed with which we come to regard whatever we encounter as routine, acceptable, and even desirable.* Even the most bizarre and unhealthy and demeaning are quickly embraced simply because they are there. Our sense of the preferred is dulled by the weight of what is laid on us, even as our sense of smell rapidly adjusts to even the foulest of odors.

On the other hand, saying "I'm OK so far" just a split second before meeting up with the reality of the ground level speaks of the *absurd slowness with which we come to accept impending change* no matter how imminent it may be. Marshall McLuhan, of course, describes this same tendency as that of seeing life through a rear-view mirror. We do not look ahead; we assume that this will protect us from the new.

An Illusion of Powerlessness

One result of not giving sufficient effort to exploring the possibilities and alternatives of the next day, year, or decade is that the illusion of powerlessness becomes almost completely operative. As a collective citizenry, we tend to be nearly paralyzed by the present. It is almost as if we, as a nation, have just begun to learn how to wiggle the big toe of the future.

Against that backdrop, we may be surprised to learn that some of us are up and running. Some have sensed the rich potential of their vision of the future, and they make it happen in their daily lives. We may have an idea that now seems impossible to achieve, but holding the idea somehow seems to give meaning to the present tense.

40 EDWARD B. LINDAMAN

Many of us envision futurism like a railroad track disappearing over the horizon, with society being the railroad car racing out of control toward the horizon, with no chance of changing its course. A much more helpful image of the future than that has been suggested by John R. Platt. He sees moving into the future as being something like a wagon train of settlers moving across the continent in an ongoing, collective search for a better place to live. There is more to come. Each one is not alone in life. Unexpected adventures await everyone. The present is illustrated by what happens when the wagon train stops at the banks of a river in, say, Wyoming, and all the pioneers sit around the fire to decide together whether to go north on the shorter route, risking being caught by winter storms, or to go in a more southerly direction, but adding at least forty days travel to the journey.

This concept may help us, for it addresses our view that life is meant to be much more than an extension of what has already happened. Who can get excited about life if life is seen as going on forever as we are now?

Connectedness . . .

We should have learned by now that we cannot talk about one thing at a time anymore. Everything connects to every other thing. We are reminded of the impact that the simple invention of the stirrup had on the development of Europe and, more recently, what the invention of the elevator safety catch by Elisha Graves Otis meant to America's landscape.

Until the simple little gadget was invented that makes it impossible for elevators to fall if their support cables should break, our cities were essentially horizontal. But with the safety catch, cities became vertical; the era of the high-rise and skyscraper was born. With spending on federal research and development in the neighborhood of twenty-five billion dollars, how many more "safety catches" will revolutionize our life-style? *

Everything is contingent on something else. Everything is relational; each thing connects, impacts some other thing. And if we are honest, we rarely know all the connections, all the kinds of impact, that any one action or invention has. Even in retrospect we may only be dealing with the tip of the iceberg.

. . . Yet Ambiguity

So ambiguity is part of our world. We can't get away from it, even as we hunger for the simple. And yet there is genuine potential for us in ambiguity. We ought to regard this phenomenon as creative ambiguity. Ambiguity can trigger personal growth just as surely as clarity. In fact, if we defined maturity as "the logic of ambiguity," we would affirm the tremendous importance in our world of having the talent or skill or character to make sense of ambiguity and to deal with it. Wringing our hands in despair is a waste of time.

---

* Mere expenditure of funds by individuals, private business, institutions or governmental agencies for research does not give us the right to sit back and wait for long sought-after breakthroughs. We can never be sure how much money, how much energy is enough. Nor can we be sure that the missing link is not in our contribution. Carl Sagan reminds us that we must, of course, exercise judgment about which applications of science to pursue but still should invest heavily in basic research:

> Without funding basic research, without supporting the acquisition of knowledge for its own sake, our options become dangerously limited. Only one physicist in a thousand need stumble upon something like the displacement of current to make the support of all thousand a superb investment for society. Without vigorous, farsighted and continuing encouragement of fundamental scientific research, we are in the position of eating our seed corn: we may fend off starvation for one more winter, but we have removed the last hope of surviving the following winter.[2]

Perhaps the most helpful beginning we can make in getting a handle on our "crazy, mixed-up world" is to recognize how closely our individual and collective destiny is connected to our awareness of what is possible.

A story about an ant in a book by Allen Wheelis helps us at this point. He writes:

> I open the door of my car and notice in a corner of vision an ant scurrying about on the smooth barren surface of the concrete parking lot, doomed to be crushed at any moment by one of the thousand passing wheels. There exists, however, a brilliant alternative for this gravely endangered creature: in a few minutes a woman will appear with a picnic basket and she and I will drive to a sunny hilltop meadow. This desperate ant has but to climb the wheel of my car to some sheltered ledge and in a half hour will be in a paradise for ants. But this option, unknown, unknowable, really yields no freedom to the ant, who is doomed; and the only irony belongs to me who observes. I reflect that options potentially as meaningful to me as this one to this ant may at this moment be eluding *my* awareness; so I too may be doomed—*this planet looks more like a parking lot every day.*[3]

Regardless of the number of options out there, we have only as much freedom as we have awareness of options. We need to cultivate thinking in terms of alternatives. Each of us can do more. For example, in our meetings or work sessions, or in our businesses, we can allocate time for consideration of what might be possible . . . if, if only we did this or that. I have found, for instance, that the time I spend each Monday with my staff at Whitworth in exploring options, and what each option might mean, is probably the most important element of our meetings.

We Can Be Futurists

One of the words that is becoming "good currency" in the late 1970's is "futurist." Although it has not been settled exactly how to express the particular label—futurology, futurism, futures studies, futuristics, etc.—there is consensus about the way a futurist approaches the future.

First, as futurists, we make explicit the assumptions we hold about the future. This is critical. One of the lessons that modern studies of human nature have taught us is that our assumptions "drag us" into the future. It works like this: every morning as we wake up, we clothe that day's behavior with certain assumptions—I'll make it to work safely, I won't get fired, I'll make a sale today, the washer and dryer will work, etc. While we cannot control all the factors affecting those activities, our assumptions predicate certain behavior. If we value planning (I'll keep 2:30 to 3 open), then it is likely we will get to it.

These assumptions, these visions of the future (even of the single, immediate day) are like magnets pulling us into the future. We all know people around us who have the knack of setting up internal magnets that pull them toward fulfillment and accomplishment. Their vision of the future empowers them in the present moment.

So the more we know about our assumptions, the better equipped we are to connect the present with the future tense.

An essential second step is to examine one's life, and the world in general, in terms of apparent trends and probable outcomes. This is the technique of scouting the terrain. We see what has already been set in motion so we can take advantage of certain aspects or brace ourselves against certain others. This can be as simple as making a self-inventory or as complex as reading profound charts that relate the past, present, and probable dimensions of consumption, growth, usage, supply, and other vital indicators.

Third, a futurist looks beyond the trends and probable outcomes to imagine other possibilities. This is the creative step—inventing one's own hopes. At this point it is important to disregard considerations of money, practicality, past failures, and other obstacles. It helps to realize that *everything that is now possible was at one time impossible.* In every case someone somewhere dared to dream, dared to imagine something a little better, a little different.

Once we have imagined how we would like the future to be—personally and, more broadly, for the world—and we stack up our ideas against what is and what is likely to be—we each need to take the value step, which is to choose what one prefers. These choices become the basis for where we want to go.

When we say "I choose this" or "I prefer that" for our future, we immediately step out of the contemplative dimension into the present tense. At this point we have to grapple with the oftentimes disturbing reality of the consequences of our present behavior on our chosen future. We may value, on one scale, close family ties and close friendships, but habits such as excessive drinking, climbing status ladders, or one-upmanship may be pushing for the opposite outcome. Adjusting our day-to-day behavior may be necessary if we are to hold faithfully to our chosen future.

A Preferred Future?

What is the risk of envisioning a preferred future for your family or for your local club? The greater risk, it seems to me, is not to take the time or make the effort that goes into that dreaming. For, by default, we are giving in to other forces and factors which may well be antithetical to our values. We should regard more seriously what an advantage it is to envision clearly what we prefer in the days, months, or years to come, for this motivates us in shaping the "right now" to eventually embrace that vision.

In reality, we approach this whole question of the future from a variety of perspectives. Some perspectives actually point us away from an open-ended examination of alternatives.

One response, perhaps less common today than in the years prior to the oil embargo and the natural-gas shortage, is to resolutely turn back to the ways of the past and try to ignore the new and impending. Similarly, we can shrug off the future by being so obsessed and involved with what we are doing right now that we never have time to consider the options. Those who place their future entirely in the hands of their religion may assume no personal responsibility for their own life, let alone their little corner of the world. To rely solely on divine intervention, it seems, is to alibi, "I don't have to do anything."

Still another means of walking away from the future is to oversimplify and insist that history repeats itself, so what's the use of getting involved? And, of course, there are cults and techniques (such as suicide) that specialize in dropping out of the future-making process altogether.

On the other hand, one can place too much trust in charts and trend lines and end up passively waiting for all the predictions to come true. This is to leap blindly into the future without making any preferences.

While strains of each of these postures may be present in all of us, our best approach is to become "hopefully involved" in the future. I see such a view as being deeply rooted in the Judeo-Christian hope for the future and belief in the potential of rebirth of the individual and of the world itself. Faith by itself deteriorates, but it is always hope that revitalizes faith. The Scriptures teach us of the "new order that begins in Christ," not as a closed and final action, but as something that continues through history.

But whether or not one accepts that premise, it does seem clear that we must be hopeful about guiding our own futures and contributing to the shaping of a collective future which we share with others.

Probing Questions

We make a good beginning in this process when we ask probing questions. The more we get into this probing—the more we *really have to know*—the more open we are to what comes in answer, even if radically new and unexpected. Some of the questions most helpful to me in establishing a clearer sense of thinking in the future tense are listed here:

• Who do we think the future is for? Is it for me, my family, the poor, the oppressed?

• Who or what is shaping my image of the future? Is it the television or your boss or your spouse? Is it your political beliefs or your economic history? Is it Buckminster Fuller or the latest pop fad?

• Is civilization as we know it today coming to an end? Is it likely to end in the sense of an atomic holocaust or in a gigantic transformation likened to the end of the Stone Age?

• How predictable is the future? What is reversible and what is not?

• Who is best prepared for the future? And where does one receive such a preparation? (I often ask students in the audiences wherever I speak if they've ever had a chance to take a course on how to live in the future. What a day it will be when finally someone raises a hand and says yes!)

Asking questions exposes us to new reality. The more

questions we are asked and the more questions we ask of others, the more we see, and the better able we are to deal with the future. A question seriously asked "sets us up" for the answer. Paul Tillich wrote that until one seriously asks the question, "Who is God?" one will never come to know him.

The future becomes increasingly important to us as we understand more clearly the consequences of some of our present actions. Many now are seeking ways to be responsible, not only for the present but also for the future.

Current visionaries do not think about static worlds, but about possibilities. (Just as there is no end to history, so there can be no limit on possible transformations.)

Tomorrow starts for you and for me with a desire for something that is said or thought to be impossible. Our everyday routine of life is hardly something to get excited about if it means that we are going on forever as we have been. We do yearn for something better, and it is always in the future.

Over the centuries the faithful seem to have had a perception of the future, the better future that at the moment seems impossible to achieve, but somehow their hopes appeared to give meaning to their present moment.

Whenever man stands on the threshold of the uncertain he hesitates. But never for long. He always proceeds. Why? Because somehow he knows that what he is doing is akin to God's purposes, and so he goes forth with his imagination linked to his action. His horizons are expanded—his static paradigms shattered.

The past is being gathered in, and present possibilities are shaking hands with the future of our vision.

As man develops his consciousness for perceiving a greater form of himself, he creates larger and grander vistas for the fulfillment of himself.[1]

I. Rice Pereira

3
"Drawing Forth of What Is Uniquely Me"

Ironically, at the very time when pessimism about the future permeates so much of popular culture, the possibility of venturing into radically new frontiers of thought and action is greater than ever before. For the first time in the history of humankind, we have the knowledge and skills to arrange, invent, and order the world we live in, rather than merely be "reactors" to a world we were thrust into at the moment of birth.

Both the Marble and the Chisel

While Environmental Impact Statements are nearly always controversial and usually frustrating to proponents of certain construction plans, the ability to project long-term results of our actions has come of age and heralds the dawn of a new future for the human race. We are now, as Heschel has said, "both the marble and the chisel." We no longer have to wait for time to pass; we are consciously building our world around us, assessing in advance such factors as energy demands, traffic flow, health hazards, and cost to the *psyche*. We deliberate over what supersonic airplanes, suburban shopping centers, and nuclear power plants will mean to us and to unborn generations. And, before long, we may enlarge the scope of our thinking to consider the advantages and disadvantages of tapping the resources beyond earth's atmosphere.

The fifty-two million square miles of land on planet Earth are the most precious real estate in the solar system. But now, thanks to the technological advances of the space age, an additional 100 million square miles—our moon, the planets Mercury and Mars, and numerous asteroids—may be considered as a readily available source of raw materials for the next century. Just when we thought that pioneering had drawn to a close, we have found new territories to explore, so vast that they dwarf our entire planet. The will to explore can be turned loose again, and it can motivate explorations into everything we do, not merely astronomical but also industrial, political, educational, social, physical, and spiritual.

"I cannot imagine a more foreboding apocalyptic vision than the future of humankind endowed with cosmic powers, but condemned to solitary confinement on one small planet," says Dr. Kraft Ehricke, space science advisor to the Space Division of Rockwell International. He has, for a number of years, been insisting that our insatiable thirst to expand, explore, and learn cannot and should not be squelched. Ehricke predicts that this urge is irreversible and will continue for centuries more. In fact, as early as 1957 just after *Sputnik,* he framed his views in terms of three fundamental laws of astronautics:

> First Law: Nobody and nothing under the natural laws of this universe impose any limitations on man except man himself.

> Second Law: Not only the earth, but the entire solar system, and as much of the universe as he can reach under the laws of nature, are man's rightful field of activity.

> Third Law: By expanding through the universe, man fulfills his destiny as an element of life, endowed with the power of reason and the wisdom of the moral law within himself.

If Ehricke is correct, we have caught barely a glimpse of the horizons ahead. The caution here is that these new horizons are not automatic; in fact they could be attainable in terms of our capability, but unattainable in terms of our attitude or willingness to move in those directions. While it would be tragic to assume that a linear progression of what we are now doing is best, it would be equally wrong to pursue everything that is technologically possible.

We face many choices in the next few years. Perhaps the strongest tension will be between the urge to expand—mining from the solar system, for example—and the urge to retrench: retard growth, simplify life-styles, conserve, recycle, and the like.

The answers are not clear, but it is certain that our thinking will be challenged as never before. How can we prepare for those decisions? What are the barriers to making wise choices and lifting our horizons?

We might begin by understanding the critical role which education has in determining how we see our world. The formal and informal systems of learning set the basic parameters of our vision. Education exists within the strong support network of cultural forces—biases and taboos, language and rewards, hopes and fears. Education is rooted in time, reflecting the past more than the present.

> Man is a venture in knowledge. The story of knowledge and its uses, good and bad, is the story of man. Man's knowledge is essentially incremental. It not only accumulates but also metabolizes and grows, feeding on other things and on itself. Its potential is unlimited, which means that when it is true as true can be, and certain beyond the shadow of a doubt, it is also incomplete.[2]

The history of knowledge and information systems, briefly sketched, looks something like this:

Only after being on earth a comparatively short time did man move from his original oral culture, in which records were unknown and unthought of, to literacy. The first script appeared around 3500 B.C. In another 2,000 years, the alphabet put in its appearance. By the mid 1400's, alphabetic letterpress printing came center stage in West Central Europe. In another 400 years, the telegraph was devised; within another sixty years, the wireless. Thirty-five more years brought television. A few decades later we have the whole panoply of spacecraft, synchronous communication satellites, and computers. Each advance exploited existing knowledge more efficiently than had the advances that went before.

We began by talking, then someone invented writing, then came printing, then came the printing press followed by mass media (volume printing, making information available cheaply and quickly), then came telegraph, radio, and television. Soon to be added to this accumulation of transmission capability will be a powerful technological convergence that makes preceding progress from oral to print to television seem incidental. When we add the computer, with its ability to store and recombine and retrieve information, to the TV, anyone with a TV set can have access to any information at will, much as is now possible at the Library of Congress. Then, when communication satellites are hooked into the television system, we can visually link the whole world together with this information. Anyone anywhere with a TV set can interrogate the computer source of information. Fully around the globe we can communicate infinite amounts of information "person to person" almost instantly.

Peter Drucker's excellent book, *Landmarks of Tomorrow,* is especially useful in helping us understand why we all experience so much dissonance in our lives. As he points out, our technology has given us a world view that is not yet taught in our schools, not yet part of our common culture.

> We still profess and we still teach the world-view of the past three hundred years. But we no longer see it. We have as yet no name for our new vision, no tools, no method and no vocabulary. But a world-view is, above all, an experience. It is the foundation of artistic perception, philosophical analysis and technical vocabulary. And we have acquired this new foundation, all of a sudden, within these last fifteen or twenty years.[3]

Our "old world view" basically holds that the whole is determined by the parts. It indicates that all of reality is causal; to know the whole, you identify the parts; to understand the behavior of the whole you find out what the parts are doing. And yet, as our discussion of physics will show and as our world has inexorably changed, we are now experiencing reality as patterns and processes.

> Every discipline has as its center today a concept of a whole that is not the result of its parts, not equal to the sum of its parts, and not identifiable, knowable, measurable, predictable, effective or meaningful through identifying, knowing, measuring, predicting, moving or understanding the parts. The central concepts in every one of our modern disciplines, sciences and arts are patterns and configurations.[3]
>
> . . . .
>
> These configurations can never be reached by starting with the parts—just as the ear will never hear a melody by hearing individual sounds. Indeed, the parts in any pattern or configuration exist only, and can only be identified, in contemplation of the whole. Just as the same sound in a tune rather than C$\sharp$ or A$\flat$, depending on the key we play in, so the parts in any configuration—whether the "drives" in a personality, the complex of chemical, electrical and mechanical actions within a metabolism, the specific rites and customs in a culture, or

the particular colors and shapes in a nonobjective painting—can only be understood, explained or even identified from their place in the whole, that is in the configuration.[5]

What are some of these processes that we experience in our everyday lives? Drucker lists some of them: automation, management, administration, political process, productivity. And he reminds us that the emphasis in speech and language itself has shifted from grammar to the whole message and its context in terms of personality, needs, and situation of the sender and receiver.

These terms and concepts are brand-new. Not a single one of them had any scientific meaning fifty years ago, let alone any standing and respectability in the vocabulary of scholar and scientist. All of them are *qualitative;* quantity in no way characterizes them. A culture is not defined by the number of people who belong to it, or by any other quantity; nor is a business enterprise defined by size. Quantitative change matters only in these configurations when it becomes qualitative transformation—when, in the words of the Greek riddle, the grains of sand have become a sand pile. This is not a continuous but a discontinuous event, a sudden jump over a qualitative threshold at which sounds turn into recognizable melody, words and motions into behavior, procedures into a management philosophy, or the atom of one element into that of another. Finally, none of these configurations is as such measurable quantitatively or capable of being represented and expressed—except in the most distorted manner—through the traditional symbols of quantitative relationships. None of these new concepts, let me emphasize, conforms to the axiom that the whole is the result of its parts. On the contrary, they all conform to a new and by no means yet axiomatic assertion, namely that the *parts exist in contemplation of the whole.*[6]

Reality is experienced as a process, and we have begun to see change as normal rather than extraordinary. So long as changes were slow and nearly imperceptible to each generation, rapid changes and growth were viewed with alarm. But when, within a single lifetime, the mode of transportation, for example, could shift from horseback and steam engine to automobile and jet and spacecraft, then the basic premise that change is unnatural had to be reexamined. This reexamination has not lessened the pain of change or produced a broad understanding of this newly discovered world. We may even take these new realities for granted without understanding them.

> Though we talk glibly of "configuration," "purpose" and "process," we do not yet know what these terms express. We have abandoned the Cartesian world-view; indeed it is rapidly becoming almost incomprehensible to us. But we have not, so far, developed a new synthesis, a new toolbox of methods, or new axioms of meaning, order and inquiry. We have certainly not yet produced a new Descartes. As a result we are in intellectual and aesthetic crisis in every area.[7]

Drucker believes that the crises of our times are symptomatic of the need to attain a new synthesis or unity of understanding. Bemoaning the specialization and complication within each specialization, Drucker reminds us that the special task of our time is to "understand *patterns* of physical, biological, psychological, and social order" as we strive for a new integration of our world view.

What is required in this integrated view and in the educational system that helps us understand and apply it?

> It must give us a concept of the "whole" as a universal and yet specific reality—whether it be "system," "organism" or "situation." We need a discipline rather than a vision, a strict discipline of qualitative and irrevocable

changes such as development, growth or decay. We need rigorous methods for anticipation of such changes. We need a discipline that *explains events and phenomena in terms of their direction and future state rather than in terms of cause*— a calculus of potential, you might say, rather than one of probability. We need a philosophy of purpose, a logic of quality and ways to measure qualitative change. We need a methodology of potential and opportunity, of turning points and critical factors, of risk and uncertainty, constant and timing, "jump" and continuity. We need a dialectic of polarity in which *unity and diversity are defined as simultaneous and necessary poles of the same essence.*

This may sound like a big order—and one we are as yet far from being able to fill. Yet we may well have the new synthesis more nearly within our grasp than we think. On it are based powers we already exercise: the power to innovate, and the power to harmonize individual and society in a new dynamic order.

If there is one thing we have learned, it is the truth of the old injunction of the seventh grade mathematics teacher: Don't worry about getting the right answer: what matters is setting up the right problem. In philosophy, science and methodology—and even more perhaps in art—a problem begins to be solved the moment it can be defined, the moment the right questions are being asked, the moment the specifications are known which the answers must satisfy. For then we know what we are looking for, what fits and what is relevant.[8]

In essence, we need to invent a new focus for our thinking. This focus sees life not in terms of causes of actions, but in terms of their direction and possible results. We are challenged to think in the future tense. This is an attitude that generates many questions about the future and a willingness to explore where the answers and lack of answers lead.

The new "axial" position around which any future educational system must work involves two concepts. The first is the almost unlimited capacity to rearrange matter, including life itself. The other is the unity of mankind on earth. Previous history placed people in scattered clusters, mutually independent. Today's history sees the whole earth as a problem and a task. Humanity now has one history. One destiny governs the whole.

We are at last able to "amen" the model for living given to us centuries ago by Seneca, the Roman philosopher. He properly connected facts to values, writing:

> The mathematician teaches me how to lay out the dimensions of my estates; but I should rather he taught me how to lay out what is enough for a man to own. He teaches me to count, and adapts my fingers to avarice; but I should prefer him to teach me that there is no point in such calculations, and that one is none the happier for tiring out the bookkeepers with his possessions. What good is there for me in knowing how to parcel out a piece of land, if I don't know how to share it with my brother?

These two factors—reshaping our world and a united human destiny—more than any other factors will shape the future of our educational system. We will most likely move toward modeling the kind of future we want, and much of the educational resources in our nation will provide the basis for planning a future worthy of human potential.

We might look ahead to the year 1998, illustrating (though speculatively) the world of change with which educators will deal during the next two decades. Obviously in the year 1998, the world will be very different from the one we know in 1978.

• Travel-time to anywhere on earth has shrunk to a matter of an hour or two.

• The International Lunar Base (Luna City) has citizen-scientists from virtually every country in the world. Sophisticated research in astronomy and geology are done cooperatively. A joint venture between Europe, the United States, and Russia has landed six men on Mars.

• A computer-based National Data Center makes technical information available in nearly every field of knowledge. Three-dimensional, holographic, color TV sets, with a hundred specialized channels, are as common in homes as telephones were in the 1970's.

• Facsimile transmission has virtually eliminated the newspaper.

• Practically everyone has a wrist-watch-size TV set, so no one is ever out of touch with what is happening in the world.

• Sophisticated learning terminals, graphic tablets, and multipurpose TV-type displays are available to students in all grades.

• The "International Remote Sensing Satellite Consortium" has been operating on a worldwide basis for more than ten years, having had its beginning in the late 1970's when information from ERTS (Earth Resources Technology Satellite) began to have its impact on the whole world. The United Nations had to develop a new cooperative program to respond to the data transmitted by a fleet of these remote sensing devices. Crop management, new mineral sources, air and water pollution are just a few of the items now requiring responsible cooperation on a worldwide basis.

• The compartmentalized public school system has been replaced by the Neighborhood Continuing Education Center, available for everyone from the very young to the very old. It is an exciting place for everyone. But with the increasing complexity of our technological society it will have become absolutely necessary for most adults to take special courses periodically in order to comprehend and adjust to the sudden changes occurring during very short periods of time—major changes coming about in the space of a year or two, instead of in five or ten.

• Computer instruction is available for all. Teachers help students to assimilate the information they receive and tie it into other facets of their lives and interests. Beginning in the early 1980's, colleges in the Pacific Northwest pioneered in the development of a Northwest Program of Airborne Instruction (NPAI), broadcasting basic courses in science and the humanities on several of the 100 cable-television channels now available to citizens for a small monthly fee.

• The classroom is a place for discussion, reflection and gaining the wisdom which makes knowledge worthwhile. There is no competition for grades, only inward fulfillment—and the thrill of knowing is the reward.

• Sea-grant colleges (similar to the land-grant colleges of the late nineteenth century) are now in full operation doing ocean engineering, aqua-mining studies, investigating ocean living possibilities, and research in ocean farming of crops and fish.

• Space-grant colleges are just coming into their own. Beginning shortly after the first space-shuttle flight in 1980, there is now an international program themed around a solar system civilization.

• Space station solar-power systems are providing half of the world's power, and there is now serious talk about mining some asteroids and sending a manned probe to the moons of Jupiter.

To attain a clear understanding of future tense and the rich potential of what might be, we must learn to be involved in thoughts that are ahead of what we already comprehend and actions that will generate new data and new questions. We can become more comfortable with not knowing all the answers, but in sensing the direction that we want to go and in moving toward the goals we have set for ourselves.

We can borrow from the religious communities around the globe who live by faith. Father William Lynch in his book, *Images of Faith,* explains that we always experience or image on the basis of expectations or hypotheses or paradigms. To a large degree, faith "patterns facts, it recomposes them in accordance with its terms." Faith precedes rather than adds to knowledge. We can venture forth on new intellectual journeys bolstered by faith. Says Lynch, "Let faith not be an old man attached at a later date to human culture and knowledge. *Let it be present at and carved as central force into the very birth of persons.*"[9]

In practical terms, what can we look for and require of our educational systems? The old world view says that we should prepare students for specific vocations. We can at least stop preparing people for occupations that are disappearing. We can go further and give all students a grasp of all branches of knowledge and modest competence in being a continuing learner. At the same time, we need to reexamine the teaching that insists upon individualism and competition over collectivism and sharing. The interrelationships of our world grow ever clearer; to ignore them is to commit economic and political suicide.

We need to take a new look at the liberal arts and humanities to appreciate what they contribute to our ability to think in the future tense. For one thing, they encompass the full scope of man's beliefs, ideals, and highest achievements and join the minds of the ages together to help us understand our universe—future as well as past and present. The humanities and liberal arts hone our ability to plan, set goals, and to work toward deliberately chosen goals rather than to be governed by urges and whims.

They help us resist dogmatism and to take joy and delight in the differences among peoples, nations, cultures, and ages. Furthermore, they nurture the spirit of dealing creatively with the uncertainties we experience and to contemplate the future with imagination and enthusiasm.

The liberal arts begin with the premise of the uniqueness of each human being. Education is a process of nurturing a person in the full breadth and depth of human potential. Education, at its essence, does not pour various mixtures of a universal brew, "truth," into mere empty vessels that happen to be variously shaped people by varying capacities. Rather, education has much more to do with helping each person to know *what* he does best, and to understand *how* he does that best. In combination with the wisdom of the ages, as illumined through the interrelated disciplines of the liberal arts, unique "me" is equipped to participate in my own creation.

Freeing me from superstition, ignorance, fear, and prejudice, education leads me to simultaneously revel in the marvels of King Tut's tomb and of walking on the moon, introduces me to the nuclei of the atom and to the opera, touches me with the tragedy of *Hamlet* and the chaos of the Bronx when Con Edison's electrical-delivery system fails. Education relates all these elements together, but keeps my uniqueness and your uniqueness at the center of it all.

From my own perspective, I would argue that the liberal arts institutions can be especially effective in bringing about the fusion of the best of the humanities (what people have done in history), technical knowledge currently available, and the sense of prophetic inquiry born of a Christian heritage and commitment. Such colleges have, in recent years, assumed a role formerly occupied by the church— answering questions about the nature and destiny of humanity and what constitutes highest value and meaning.

As we go about the difficult task of refocusing our thinking, we might evaluate each of the following ten guidelines for an educational experience that opens the way to new personal and corporate frontiers:

1. We are, each one, a child of God, living under the authority of the Creator. As such, we are to be responsible, mature, hopeful planners, and participators in God's world.

2. We seek to discover and nurture the creative talent that exists in each person because each one is created in the image of God.

3. We make intelligent use of our world, God's creation; we become thankful users rather than thoughtless consumers.

4. We have created an artificial, man-made urban environment where fully 80 percent of the world's population lives, and we work diligently at making urban life more rewarding, more fulfilling to the human spirit.

5. We work cooperatively with other people around the world for human betterment. We see ourselves as interdependent. We recognize the need for love in the world.

6. We strive to implant the quest for self-improvement as a lifelong preoccupation; the tools for efficient self-learning are readily available in computers and related hardware and software.

7. We remove obstructions to understanding how politics and economics work; if people truly are sovereign and can govern themselves, they need more than partial truths and sketchy highlights to make decisions. By necessity mass media oversimplifies. Education must fill in the gaps.

8. We must develop our critical intelligence and the self-respect and confidence to use it.

9. We cultivate an openness that permits contemplation

of all ideas for human betterment, no matter how odd or radical they may seem at the outset. We welcome different viewpoints and approaches.

10. We value learning and help others acquire this value for themselves. We work to inspire others to care about theirs and others' growth in knowledge and understanding. We begin to see that helping others develop is a survival tactic.

But these guidelines must fit within the framework of an overriding philosophy of life, or we risk that they will simply be a kind of vacuous, intellectual popcorn. These ideals, a set of assumptions based on facts and values, constitute a moral and intellectual force that is as weak or as strong as our own self-image. If you or I were to be stripped to the very essence of self, I wonder if we would find power or powerlessness there.

I believe that those who, in the last analysis, are powerless or who believe themselves to be, fail to see that the ability to invent one's future rests on two points: (1) That God is at work through our lives, and (2) Creative energy flows out of the intermixing of knowledge and information with the unique person that each one of us is. When knowledge is linked to unique self, then something creative, something new, something of God happens. Education addresses this critical ingredient of what we know; *it calls us out of ourselves and into the world.*

The formula goes something like this: I am unique, and I acknowledge that God is working through me, through my feelings and my talents, and that when these are connected to what I *know*—including what I know of my neighbors and their needs—I constitute a one-of-a-kind creative force.

A fictional psychiatrist named Dr. Broderick captures

this idea in a talk he gives to the residents of Jefferson House, in a book, *Jefferson House,* soon to be published by Robert K. Greenleaf.

> The most important lesson I have learned about maturity is that the emergence, the full development, of what is uniquely *me* should be an important concern throughout my entire life. There are many other important concerns but this particular one must never be submerged, never be out of sight.

> This I learned the hard way. There was a long "wilderness" period in which I sought resources outside myself. I looked for an "answer" to the normal frustrations of life. Good years went by. No answers came. It took me a long time to discover that the only real answer to frustration is to concern myself with *drawing forth of what is uniquely me.* [Lindaman's italics] Only as what is uniquely me emerges do I experience moments of true creativity; moments which, when deeply felt, temper the pain of long periods of frustration that are the common lot of most of us and give us the impulse and the courage to act constructively in the outside world.[10]

If I were asked what was Christopher Columbus' greatest achievement in discovering America, my answer would not be that he took advantage of the spherical shape of earth to get to India by the western route—this idea had occurred to others before him—or that he prepared his expedition meticulously and rigged his ships most expertly—that, too, others could have done equally well. His most remarkable feat was the decision to leave the known regions of the world and to sail westward, far beyond the point from which his provisions could have got him back home again.[1]

Werner Heisenberg

4
"I Think, Therefore I . . ."

People of all cultures tend to identify with the heroic. The individual who defies the logic of the time and flies in the face of certain defeat and somehow emerges triumphant is celebrated far and wide. Our spirits are lifted by those few who prove that the limits we all struggle against may, in fact, be transcended.

Our common mistake, however, is to let the heroic example rest at the level of an emotionally satisfying symbol. The psychic or spiritual uplift that we enjoy from another's heroic act too often is a temporary balm, an aspirin that momentarily makes the pain of an out-of-control world less severe. On the other hand, for some the inspiration leads to purposeful activity. The emotional surge is accompanied by a willingness to examine the apparent "miracle" to discern how one might achieve a similar breakthrough. And there is an energizing that eventually issues in unexpected acts of courage probing beyond the known, discovering new truths.

Limited by Perception

Sadly, we are imprisoned by the limits of our mental perceptions of what is real or logical or possible. Only occasionally do we seriously examine the "facts"—boundaries we chafe against; if we did we would frequently discover only suppositions based on what formerly had been accepted as true. The logic that holds us in "our place" may well be "good logic" that is based on erroneous assumptions. But we rarely find this out.

While it is interesting to speculate on the reasons why humankind does not demonstrate more hope or more courage, my purpose here is to examine how our view of the world limits our lives. This phenomenon is clearly revealed in an examination of how human comprehension has changed in the past few centuries.

The nonscientific-minded may be surprised to learn that it is through the history of physics that we can best understand how our mental picture of reality and our behavior are closely linked together. Physics is derived from the Greek word, *physis,* which originally meant "the endeavor of seeing the essential nature of things." [2] We pick up the story in the fifth century B.C., when the idea of the atom was first conceived.

Development of Thought Processes

Greek philosophers, wrestling with the notion of the nature of the world, developed the idea of the atom, the smallest indivisible unit of matter, as distinct from spirit. As Fritjof Capra writes in *The Tao of Physics,*

> The Greek atomists drew a clear line between spirit and matter, picturing matter as being made of several 'basic building blocks.' These were purely passive and intrinsically dead particles moving in the void. The cause of their motion was not explained, but was often associated with external forces which were assumed to be of spiritual origin and fundamentally different from matter.[3]

The scientific study of matter was a long time in coming. During the subsequent two thousand years, Western thought followed the lead of Aristotle who systematized the study of the spiritual dimension—the nature of God, the nature of man, good and evil, and other subjects related to the "soul."

By the seventeenth century, this dualistic view of the world had taken on strict formulations. French philosopher-scientist René Descartes described nature as having two separate and independent realms—mind and matter. This compartmentalization elevated consciousness, the rational, and the intellect while relegating the material world to the state of "dead" pieces of a gigantic machine ruled from above by a monarchical God. Descartes' foundational position—"I think, therefore I am"—placed the mind at center stage. And for the most part Western man ever since has equated his identity with his mind. The mind's connection with the rest of the body—with all of matter—is distant, according to this perspective.

Within this philosophical framework, classical physics was about to flower. Three hundred years ago the brilliant scientist Sir Isaac Newton led the way in formulating an expanding understanding of how the world works. Newton's mechanical model of the universe stood unchallenged until this century, and even though science has moved on to a much more comprehensive model, Newtonian theories became the foundation of both scientific and popular understanding of the physical world.

As school children we were introduced to the Newtonian view with the story of his being conked on the head by a falling apple (his observation and musing issued in his famous law of universal gravitation). In fact, his investigation of gravity did begin with watching apples fall, and it led him to calculate about the nature of gravitational force—not only on earth, but the moon and planets as well. His mathematical calculations agreed with astronomical observations and "at one stroke, he swept aside all the erroneous notions, held over a period of twenty centuries, about an imminent difference between things on earth and in the heavens. Where all others had failed, he succeeded in constructing a rational celestial mechanics; and he showed that the motions of both celestial and terrestial bodies are governed by the same laws." [4]

Earlier, Newton had revised the Aristotelian view that the natural state of all bodies is the state of rest. His first law of motion accurately described the effect of friction on moving bodies, and his second law of motion described the forces needed to cause, alter, or stop movement.

These laws formed the simple foundation for an understanding of a mechanical universe where everything that occurs is the direct consequence of what happened before. The unbroken chain of cause and effect was said to be observable and easily understood. Experimentation verified the hypotheses. The result was a surging of confidence that the physical world could be absolutely understood in terms of fixed laws. "In the Newtonian view, God had created, in the beginning, the material particles, the forces between them, and the fundamental laws of motion. In this way, the whole universe was set in motion and has continued to run ever since, like a machine, governed by immutable laws." [5]

To be sure, this view of reality is familiar and comfortable in our time. The Newtonian world is gears and pulleys and levers. This is the world of our senses. We can weigh objects, calibrate volume and distance, apply pressure, turn a dial, flip a switch. *This world made sense, and we assumed it was absolutely correct and the final word on natural phenomena.*

But science and the technological changes it spawned soon led to modifications of the Newtonian perspective. Investigations into the nature of electric and magnetic activity posed results which the mechanical model did not adequately explain. The work of Michael Faraday with electrical current and magnets began to concentrate attention not only on the effects (mechanical) of electromagnetism but also on the forces and the force fields. The positive

and negative charges were not rigidly connected as Newton's laws suggested; the electrical field "had its own reality
and could be studied without any reference to material
bodies." [6]

While most scientists at first tried to explain their growing knowledge of this new world—radio waves, light waves,
X rays, etc.—in mechanical terms, the walls of the Newtonian mental prison had been dented. It remained for Albert
Einstein fifty years later, at the dawn of the twentieth century, to lead physics over that wall to an understanding of relativity. And, in a separate development, an international group of scientists extended the mechanical
view of reality in still another direction—quantum mechanics.

The notion of absolute space and time, a world of ele-
mentary solid particles, and simple cause and effect was
shattered by the scientific developments of the past four
decades. The following simplified sketch of the theory of
relativity and then quantum mechanics is presented so we
might better grasp the opportunities which this new understanding of our world offers to us.

Einstein, working alone, investigated the differences between the mechanical theories of classical physics and the
newer theory of electrodynamics. He succeeded in unifying
the apparently opposing schools but, in so doing, made
major changes in the traditional concepts of the Newtonian
world view. In 1905, Einstein's special theory of relativity
was published. The importance of his famous equation,
$E = mc^2$, was primarily that the old understanding of mass
as "dead" particles—small, solid, indestructible, passive—
was irrevocably altered. Mass is nothing but a form of
energy, Einstein said, and even at rest an object has energy
stored in its mass. The "c" of the theory, the speed of
light, was the constant. But there was no absolute time,
no absolute space. In linking space and time, Einstein explained that

Different observers will order events differently in time if they move with different velocities relative to the observed events. In such a case, two events which are seen as occurring simultaneously by one observer may occur in different temporal sequences for other observers. All measurements involving space and time thus lose their absolute significance.[7]

Einstein extended his theory in 1915 with his proposal of the general theory of relativity. In this instance, his theory dealt with Newton's law of gravity, stating that the force of gravity has the effect of "curving" space and time. This has been illustrated by different outcomes of drawing a square on a two-dimensional plane and a three-dimensional sphere. The curvature of the sphere of planets and other large objects, caused by the gravitational field, means that "space around it is curved and the degree of curvature depends on the mass of the object." [8] Furthermore, since time is linked to space in this theory, it too is affected by the size of the mass where it is measured in the universe.

The difficulty with understanding the theory of relativity is that it does not readily relate to everyday experience. Astronomers observing and measuring light in the galaxies and physicists studying electrons in the laboratory have verified this new "relativistic mechanics." But while we cannot experience this phenomena in our daily lives, science and technology (where theories really begin to impact the populace) have leapfrogged to new frontiers with this new understanding of our universe.

The second major extension of the Newtonian world view wears the label, "quantum mechanics." Einstein, through his work with electromagnetic radiation, gave impetus to the study of the "submicroscopic realm of the atoms" by a number of scientists from Europe and America.[9] It happened that, as new scientific instruments allowed experimentation with electricity and light, these findings did not square with the laws of classical physics which applied so readily to large, directly observable objects. The change in scale from dust particles to X ray waves, according to the mechanical theories, should not make any difference.

Yet, for example, scientist Ernest Rutherford's study of radiation indicated that atoms were not hard and solid, as had been believed. Instead, "the atoms turned out to consist of vast regions of space in which extremely small particles—the electrons—moved around the nucleus, bound to it by electric forces." [10] By now, scientists were exploring the previously unseen microworld. The size of the atom being studied was about one hundred millionth of a centimeter. The atom could not be observed, but its behavior could be tracked with increasingly sophisticated equipment. And instead of finding subatomic units of matter to be solid, scientists learned that they were both particles and waves, depending on how they were observed.

The concept of quantum mechanics began with the discovery by German theoretical physicist Max Planck that the energy of heat radiation is emitted in "energy packets" rather than flowing continuously. These packets were dubbed "quanta" by Einstein, and quantum has come to refer to the special properties of atomic physics. What are these properties?

> At the subatomic level, matter does not exist with certainty at definite places, but rather shows 'tendencies to exist,' and atomic events do not occur with certainty at definite times and in definite ways, but rather show "tendencies to occur." In the formalism of quantum theory, these tendencies are expressed as probabilities and are associated with mathematical quantities which take the form of waves.

. . . .

Quantum theory has thus demolished the classical concepts of solid objects and of strictly deterministic laws of nature. At the subatomic level, the solid material objects of classical physics dissolve into wave-like patterns of probabilities, and these patterns, ultimately, do not represent probabilities of things, but rather probabilities of interconnections. A careful analysis of the process of observation in atomic physics has shown that the *subatomic particles have no meaning as isolated identities, but can only be understood as interconnections between the preparation of an experiment and the subsequent measurement.* Quantum theory thus reveals a basic oneness of the universe. It shows that we cannot decompose the world into independently existing smallest units. As we penetrate into matter, nature does not show us any isolated "basic building blocks," but rather *appears as a complicated web of relations between the various parts of the whole.*[11]

One of the easiest to understand expressions of this interrelatedness is the chemist's periodic table of elements. Scientists learned that the number of electrons in the atoms of an element determine its properties. The basic element is the lightest atom, hydrogen. Other elements—now more than two hundred have been identified—are attained by adding protons and neutrons to the hydrogen nucleus, and it is the *interactions between the atoms* that are observed as various chemical processes. This interaction is the basis of all solids, liquids, and gases, the basis of all living organisms and their biological processes.

The complexity of relativity theory and the subatomic world—nuclei, electron, proton, neutron, meson, neutrino, and the like—taxes the understanding of even specialist scientists. Exploring the subatomic realm has been and continues to be a baffling business, full of paradoxes which cannot be explained in the language or laws of classical science. Arthur Koestler, writing in *The Roots of Coincidence,* notes that "the deeper the physicist intruded into

the realms of the sub-atomic and super-galactic dimensions, the more intensely he was made aware of their paradoxical and common-sense-defying structure, and the
more open-minded he became towards the possibility of
the seeming impossible." [12] After half a century of research, "neither our intuition nor our language can deal
with this (four dimensional space-time character of the
subatomic world) . . . very well." [13]

The list of subatomic mysteries is very long; it ranges
from the indeterminancy of the atomic (the more accurately an elecron's location is known the more uncertain
its velocity becomes and vice versa) to complementarity
(an event viewed through two different frames of reference
which mutually exclude each other but also complement
each other and only the juxtaposition of these frames truly
describes the phenomena).

While this new science was knocking the props out from
under the smug confidence that in time the complete nature of our world could be reduced to simple laws, it was
introducing a valuable new idea that nature might not be
at all factual and certain. "The fact is that in our time
nature *has* been found to have an aspect not noticed before,
namely, indeterminancy. Thus, for whatever reasons, nature's micro-entities *cannot* be specified or measured without uncertainty. Nature simply is this way vis-a-vis men
as its observer." [14]

Even as knowledge of the subatomic is substantial, scientists have not yet framed a complete theory of nuclear
particles. Quantum and relativity theory still have not yet
been reconciled into a complete theory of the particle
world.

The Message?

What does all of this tell us about our "mental prisons"
and what we can do to get beyond their confines? Surely,

as laypersons we don't have to understand relativity and quantum physics to expand the horizons of life. Yet, we can at least recognize that as long as we wear the "mechanical glasses" of the Newtonian perspective, we are seeing a world that is comprised of things that operate mechanically. In so doing we are ignoring what science has shown us of the microworld and the unseen nature of things. Here we discover a universe that is relational, not mechanical—that is process, not thing. This should point us in the direction of viewing how the parts of our world fit together into unified systems, seeing the interconnectedness of the various realms, taking a holistic perspective about everything from earth's complex ecosystem to the mental, physical, and spiritual health of *Homo sapiens.*

Similarly, we can get more comfortable with the limits of our senses and mental frames of reference while recognizing in paradox, mystery, and ambiguity the richness of unexplored territories and new opportunities for breakthroughs.

Technological improvements in the past century have exploded the old notion that through our senses we can know all truth if we but search diligently enough. Telescope, microscope, and oscilloscope have instead revealed contradiction and exception and layer upon layer of new realities. In each case, the limits to new understanding are highly complex.

Restricted by Senses

On the one hand, we are restricted by the reach of physical senses. The eye, for example, tells us just a small fraction about the phenomena of light waves. We cannot with our eyes discern that it is ultraviolet light that causes sunburn; our eyes tell us only about visible light, and little of that is precise data. Yet with instruments of quantum mechanics we know that the photoelectric differences of light forms are largely a matter of different wave lengths and correlated differences in photon energy.

. . . But Augmented

But, as we have discovered, our senses can be augmented with technology to give us a more comprehensive view of our world. The more difficult barrier has to do with how we think. We are constricted by "beliefs, conceptions, or mythical understandings as to the nature of reality." [15] Time and time again throughout life we can be exposed to new ideas without even the slightest notice. Even the best scientists struggle with the blindness of mind-set. As Einstein remarked to Werner Heisenberg, the German physicist credited with devising the first coherent formulation of quantum mechanics, *"It is the theory which decides what we can observe."* [16]

Social scientists have helped us realize that for the most part we see what we expect to see and are closed to the unexpected.

> Perception is a two-way active process rather than a one-way passive one. Thus seeing involves much more than simply opening one's eyes. It takes place when, on the one hand, the observer, having opened his eyes, receives light from an object, and when, on the other hand, he reaches out to that object conceptually to grasp what can be seen of it. The process is then a receiving and a taking. And knowledge is both a product of perception and a frame of reference or a probe which makes perception and conception possible. In other words, what we *do see* is determined to a considerable extent by what we *have seen and conceived* and by what we suppose or believe *can be seen*. It is amazing how difficult it is at times to see—say, through a microscope—what one does not expect to see, and how easy it is to see what one does expect, even though it may not be there to be seen.[17]

We are best equipped to make the most of the data that we confront when we are not fearful of complexity, when we welcome paradox and ambiguity as signposts of potential breakthroughs to new understanding. Again, the history of the growth of quantum mechanics illustrates how new insights can ensue from probing into the seeming contradictions of life. Until the 1920's, scientists almost unanimously agreed that everything in the universe was made of particles, and so it was natural that the first sub-atomic research revealed a particulate nature. Then new experiments revealed that atoms and even molecules had the properties of waves. Gradually physicists began to describe atoms in terms of both particles and waves, without understanding how they could be both.

Harold K. Schilling, writing in *The New Consciousness in Science and Religion,* explains that the paradox was resolved when it was understood that the old imagery and concepts of the mechanical world could not possibly describe the strange new phenomena of the microworld. With the help of analogy and symbols, particularly the mathematical symbols of quantum mechanics, new symbolization evolved that allowed "a genuine expansion of human consciousness and insight—as well as momentous and sophisticated refinement of scientific methodology." [18] Yet, he reminds us that paradoxes are not the result of "transient incongruity in the nature of reality," but are produced by man's rigid habits of thought and the limitations of "language, which in turn result from his limited experience and from his reluctance to accept nonconventional implications of new experience." [19]

Since so many of life's experiences seem to make little sense and we are often confronted with ambiguity, we might benefit by digging more assertively into "the mess" rather than shrugging our shoulders and shutting our eyes. Heisenberg, late in life when he was recalling the tortuous journey to understanding the atom, remembered telling his fellow scientists at one point that they were like "a sailor, marooned on a remote island where conditions differ radically from anything he has ever known and where, to make things worse, the natives speak a completely alien tongue. He simply must make himself understood, but has no means of doing so. In that sort of situation a theory cannot 'explain' anything in the usual strict scientific sense of the word. All it can hope to do is to reveal connections and, for the rest, leave us to grope as best we can." [20]

One can devise and test possible solutions with the hope of finding a "connection" to new meanings. We are helped in such situations by taking the more objective approach of framing our ideas as possibilities rather than facts and seeing our hypotheses as "an intermediate stage between the possible and the actual." [21]

Another significant lesson in the new but incomplete understanding which relativity and quantum mechanics have given us is that we have a dramatic picture of how human understanding of truth is bound to culture and history. Truth, as postulated by Aristotle, Kant, Descartes, Newton, Einstein, or anyone, is never final and complete. It is always relative to the extent of knowledge available at the moment. This does not mean that the mechanical principles espoused by Newton are inoperable, for they do describe how much of our observable environment works. On the other hand, the new laws are more comprehensive, giving us a more accurate picture of why nature is as it is. Quite simply, the classical laws seem to "describe *how* things behave but contain no hint of *why* they do so." [22] Relativity and quantum mechanics help us get underneath the appearance of nature and give us an understanding of *why*. With these theories and modern technology, we have reached out to the stars and we have reached inside the atom. We are still discovering the incredible complexity, and yet simplicity, of our universe.

The whole direction of human thought and investigation

has turned to the depth dimension of things. Thanks to new theory and its gleanings, we have begun to probe the inner reality of nature, finding tremendously different depths and levels with distinctive qualities. While these new depths of knowledge have opened the door to atomic and hydrogen weaponry—for example, they simultaneously opened the way to atomic medicine, space exploration, lasers, and other "great new insights, powerful new modes of thought, and quite new intuitions and feelings about reality, for instance, those about its holistically relational and developmental character, that have expanded and enriched human experience so immeasurably." [23]

Each one of us is a benefactor of an enriched understanding of how and why our universe—including human beings—function. The dread of a deterministic, mechanical world of absolute cause and effect has been replaced by the hope of a world of mystery, paradox, wonder, and awe. We have only to mentally reach out and embrace this new pair of "glasses" and apply these perceptions to the setting of new heights of personal and professional goals.

Equipped with these new attitudes and tools, we take on the identity of the hero rather than merely identify with him. Embracing a relational world of processes, we "discern the vast wealth of reality in its interior depths beneath its surface features. It means also coming to understand the directly visible, at least in part, through the indirectly discernible depths within. To see in depth is also to see both quality and quantity, and to see them in balance as inseparable and complementary aspects of reality. It means being prepared to accept the utterly novel and unexpected, and even the seemingly incredible or paradoxical, and to think about them imaginatively and even unconventionally if necessary." [24]

We shall never cease from exploration, and the end of all our exploration will be to arrive where we started and to know the place for the first time.[1]

T. S. Eliot

Man not only lives on a physical plane in a world of nature, but also in a world impregnated with profound and mysterious forces. These forces evoke deep feelings in the heart of man and ignite his soul with questions to which his intuition tries to provide the answers. [Lindaman's emphasis] *These inquiries flame up into the light and bring with them the darkness before creation. Man's senses are aroused by these "unknowns." They challenge his imagination as though holding the key which may unlock his secret hopes, his desires, his aspirations; always leading him on in the quest for knowledge. These elements of Being partake of divine essence. They are veiled by their nature of being "unknowable."*[2]

I. Rice Pereira

81

5
Seeing the World for the
First Time, Each Time

One of life's most fulfilling moments occurs in that split second when the familiar suddenly is transformed into the dazzling aura of the profoundly new. These are the mountaintop experiences of life, the "come-to-life" precious times when we discover a truth, when the light bulbs of the mind suddenly glow, illuminating unexpected treasure-filled rooms. This is what is meant by the expression, "We see the world for the first time, each time."

Mired in the Mundane

Of course these breakthroughs are too infrequent, more uncommon than common; and we are mired most of the time in the mundane and trivial. The shocker: What seems mundane and trivial is the very stuff that discovery is made of. The only difference is our perspective, our readiness to put the pieces together in an entirely new way and to see patterns where only shadows appeared just a moment before.

If you have ever, as an adult, gone back to where you grew up, you have probably experienced this phenomenon. In my case, I had been away from the little Iowa town forty years before I knocked on the door of the house I had lived in from age five to fifteen. What a surprise! The bedroom that had seemed so large to me then was really just a small cubicle, and the old water tower that I remembered as being about twenty stories high was little taller than our house. No, it had not shrunk; I had grown.

Wouldn't it be fantastic if each of us might, every now and then, walk into our homes and offices and see them as if for the first time? But we are untrained in seeing potential in the relics of every day. We stand numb at unseen doors. Each of us walks Mr. Magoo-like through life, only occasionally stumbling over a fact that had been in full view for a long time.

Awareness

The secret is awareness. We can attune our sensitivity to the issues and events of our everyday to pick out those that are rich in potential and deserving of focused attention and investigation. We can learn from the Kansas farmer who stood in his corn field in 1862 watching first as work crews installed twin ribbons of steel, and then as a steam-belching great iron horse loomed into view and thundered along the tracks. He thought he saw the first train crossing the Kansas prairies. He might also have cursed the crazy world and its strange contraptions.

But look what he *did not* see: He did not see Chicago—its gigantic stockyards, its burgeoning industry, the beehive of The Loop, the Sears Building, or the linking up with the railroads to the West Coast. He did not see California, did not see the opening up of the new frontiers of the entire West.

I am suggesting that we can apply this example to our lives today. What did Americans see in the summer of 1977 when the network news shows reported a jumbo jet lumbering into the air with the test-model of our space shuttle riding piggyback for its first aerodynamic tests? Most who watched that news film merely saw a strange sight—one plane riding atop another. Some undoubtedly grumbled about the "waste of taxpayers' money." What did we fail to see? What Chicago, what Western frontier did we miss?

In chapter 1, I outlined some of the new options which this space-age "clipper ship" opens up for us—making space an economically attractive frontier for industry, energy production, and new knowledge. This "new continent" offers tremendous potential—zero gravity, vacuum, cold, sterility, all qualities beneficial to manufacturing and processing.

Island One

Consider what just one project, something known as Island One, now a think-tank concept, might mean: Island One would use the space shuttle and a yet-to-be-designed "space tug" to economically boost to that point between the moon and the earth, where our planet's gravitational pull is just slightly less than the moon's gravitational pull, a small industrial space station capable of housing up to 200 people.

Island One's basic task will be to serve as a sun-powered foundry for using moon rocks as the raw material for the metals needed to build a huge space station serving up to 10,000 people, which would then generate and transmit all the electricity needed on this planet. The technology exists to do all this. The question mark is our willingness to pay for it. The price tag is something like 600 to 1,000 billion dollars!

Before that is rejected as impossible, we should realize that this dollar figure is about what we could spend in the next twenty or thirty years right here on this planet in mining, drilling, building new power plants, and the like to produce the additional energy needed. Only on earth we are talking about energy that once used is gone forever.

We should not make too much of this think-tank idea, but the impact of an Island One—if implemented—would not be just production of "guilt-free" energy. This new "colony" in the sky would likely be populated by people of all nations, races, and backgrounds. We can only ask what would this require of us and what it would do to our religions, life-styles, and forms of government. It boggles the mind.

We do not know the answers; we can only speculate, and through such speculation we are inventing the future. This is not to indicate that these visions of the future will not be borne out in fact some day. One of the obstacles to "seeing through" and "seeing anew" is that we become so involved with our wondrous inventions. Our latest "fad toys" are small home computers that make our TV screens versatile recreational and educational display terminals. Obsessed with wanting, acquiring, and using, we may miss the implications and bridges to meaning that are in plain sight. However, as many of our leading writers, teachers, and scientists are telling us, we have already been transformed; our inventions have changed the world and, in turn, we have been changed. Even without our knowing it, our consciousness has been expanded.

Lightning and Thunder

William Irwin Thompson provocatively states that "the time has come; the revelation has already occurred, and the guardian seers have seen the lightning strike the darkness we call reality. And now we sleep in the brief interval between the lightning and the thunder." [3]

This image transports each of us in a different direction. What is the lightning? What is the thunder? Is lightning a flash of consciousness and thunder new action in that bigger world? Lightning may be seeing what is possible, being exposed to a whole new set of possibilities. Such a watershed moment in history occurs differently in each life, although it may be simultaneous—ignited by a spectacular event in history that touches millions of lives. However

perspective of a new realism about the limits of the earth and needs of humanity.[9]

A major premise of the industrial age is that the goals of society are known and agreed upon. Hence, nearly all discussion—the endless succession of meetings, conferences, briefings—is devoted to discovering how best to achieve these objectives. But many people today, particularly the young, are not buying that. They are saying that *some* of the current goals (social, political, and economic) are inappropriate for our new circumstances and need to be rethought. The purpose is not to point fingers of blame but to stimulate our thinking anew about societal goals, to admit that many of the goals are uncertain, and to reexamine them in view of the "lightning" of our recent past.

This new thinking, the reexamining of goals, might not be the kind of rational, logical, deductive style of inquiry so favored in modern times. We have benefited enormously from the precision and cold, statistical analyses of deduction, but we may now need to give more attention to the "sense" of things. Instead of arguing over the phrasing and punctuation, we can attune ourselves to the sense of the whole idea or goal. The inefficiency of this style of thinking—likened more to brainstorming than fact-finding—may make us rather uncomfortable. Yet if we are to "move from sleep to thunder" we will have to value not always being clear what we are talking about. The infant discovers language by babbling. As adults we can babble through plays, poetry, art, friendships, involvements, reading, and prayer. It is only when we are somewhat out of our depth that we reach new levels of understanding.

Growth of Consciousness

We need to better understand how our consciousness (what we see, what we think we see, and what we do because

of that) has grown over the past few centuries. I. Rice
Pereira, the late artist of international reputation, has
traced the history of consciousness from primitive to modern man to demonstrate that the degree of perception
of the world "out there" is closely linked to the inner
vistas of self. Some of the points made in this excellent
metaphysical essay, *The Nature of Space,* may help us understand what is happening to us as we try to "get a handle"
on the rapidly changing world:

1. Consciousness is multidimensional. *One-dimensional
consciousness* occurs as the mind begins to differentiate
among shape, number, and distance. At this point we
"adopt an attitude, as well as a sensory feeling, toward
outer visual experience" and even after the object passes
beyond the "framework of optical reference, there is an
imprint of the picture in the space of the mind." Then
as "the space or place of orientation and relationships
spreads out horizontally (in line), the mind spreads out
to record and imprint these spaces of memory. The more
man is able to apprehend and develop his outer experience of the sense world, the more his inner consciousness
expands." [10]

2. *Two-dimensional consciousness* develops once we begin
to make comparisons and assign meaning or values to experience. At this point we can sum up past experience.
Man, says Pereira, is then:

> . . . able to live in the physical present with a sense
> of the historical past. His memory patterns have devel-
> oped on a horizontal plane. He has a feeling-sensation
> of the world in which he lives, and this stimulates his
> capacity for thinking. Man can then look above to the
> heavens with less fear—start to ask questions—dare to
> inquire. As he activates the heights with his questions
> and inquiries, he stimulates his depths of feeling and
> intuition.

When man reaches the position from which he can inquire, the vertical comes into experience.

. . . .

As man learns to inquire into the vertical, he establishes a deeper feeling in relation to the meaning of life. These stimuli set a religious feeling in motion, because man has evoked unknown qualities and properties in space. Man's consciousness expands the more his perceptions reach out into the unknown space of the heavens and inquires.

As his outer visual picture of the world becomes larger, the mind keeps going back in time, summing up, reconstructing, distilling and refining these memory patterns, until the mind succeeds in developing images of the world, and eventually extracts essences from these images. In this process, the world of physical space becomes smaller, as the mind re-adapts its impressions, and the capacity to grasp symbolic, mathematical space becomes greater. The more man is able to absorb of his physical world, the more the mind sums up. The outer visual horizontal picture of the world contracts, as the inner experience of the vertical becomes deeper, until the mind is able to contain a two-dimensional linear pattern.[11]

3. When the mind begins to devise a system of measurement (mathematics) and can represent nature accurately with pictures (art), *three-dimensional consciousness* is attained. Now we are able to measure space as distance and meter time by the clock. Historically, this precipitated the great leap into the industrial age. People became preoccupied with machinery, with objects. "Intuition and feeling became more and more submerged as man travelled the external world of invention, building instruments of mechanical perfection, and attempting to make mechanics the foundation of all knowledge." [12]

4. As human knowledge expands, and as "direct observation is limited to an infinitely small portion of physical

space, the discrepancy between the outer optical appearances of things, and the nature of the substance contained in the thing perceived, becomes manifest." What happens, explains Pereira, is that when *feeling and thinking become separated* we experience life as "flat"; consciousness is unreal to us—it has no inner representation. And when we are unable to give our "experience of the three-dimensional world inner solidarity, there will be a contraction of space" when we are "confronted with the irrational, incomprehensible realm of the infinitely large. . . ." The result? We sense a "void" and "chaos," and we become anxious, filled with fear and dread.[13]

5. Consciousness is a process of making space in the mind—representing concrete, objective things in physical space in a conceptual, symbolic space—which requires active participation in life. The world of things is sensory, tactile, a kinetic field of action. But our perceptions are spatial, ranging far beyond physical realities. These qualities transcend rational thought; we are intuitive, spiritual beings. And it is when intuition, thought, and feeling are united with the object of experience that we attain what Pereira calls *four-dimensional* consciousness:

> If man continues to live on a horizontal plane, unconscious of space-time, there will be no discrepancy between what he thinks and what he feels, since what he experiences is confined to, and corresponds with, the visual appearance of things and the sense data of objective reality. *But, should his intuition and feeling become activated by the new concept of his universe, the contradictions immanent in his old world-view will become manifest.* [Lindaman's Italics]

> In space-time the horizontal, material world of matter must be joined with the concept of substance. The concept of substance lies within the vertical plane of intuition, thought and feeling and must be united with the

object of experience. In this way, the outer world of sensory appearances, and the inner sensation of the thing perceived, merge simultaneously in the mind through the image which cognition makes possible. This gives volume and depth to experience and releases energy from the concrete, static, inert object fixed in space.

Although the object can never be completely known, the mind has the potentiality of illuminating the object of experience so that it can be referred to the intelligence for cognition and thus be made intelligible to consciousness. Therefore, the energy contained in the space which was once occupied by the object is liberated and made available for the structure of consciousness.

The apprehension of space and the development of human consciousness are parallel. The more energy that is illuminated and redeemed from the substance of matter, the more fluid the perceptions become and the more the mind sums up into abstraction. The mind's capacity for dimensionality and the structure of consciousness become available through experiencing one's own action. Illumination can take place only through the subject knowing himself first. There is no object unless the subject participates in his own experience. One cannot explore a dimension unless the constellation of one's own consciousness is prepared to apprehend it.[14]

6. Consciousness that *merges the horizontal plane with the vertical* acquires a creative, deepening, forward-moving quality of mind energy. Wholeness, then, is a characteristic describing a unification of awareness, perception, cognition, intuition, and feeling which generates tremendous energy. Pereira believes the energy is created in symbolically expressing what we sense and feel of the unknown:

. . . only that portion of . . . energy which one is able to adapt to the reality representing the known limitations of the world, has the potential of being utilized objectively. The remaining portion, belonging to the unknown content, is expressed symbolically. The creative source of this core of energy eternally tries to transcend the limitations of the known boundaries and to open up vistas into an ever-expanding horizon, seeking new knowledge.

This unifying system binds feeling and thinking and relates them to the senses and intuition. Intuition provides either sign, signal or symbol for reconciling this energy to reality. On a two-dimensional plane, the mind functions by sign. When the mind functions by sign, it must depend on facts, reason, and the object—signs of the times: and, on a primitive level, relies on instinct and superstition. In a three-dimensional sense, the mind is able to form the image—or we can say signal—by which the inner and outer are merged, producing a simultaneous experience. In a four-dimensional world, the mind has the capacity for dimensionality and extension in space through the symbol.[15]

7. As consciousness, through symbols, links the known with the unknown, it also converts symbols into objective representations—new behavior, new expressions. However, not much of the symbolic dynamic can be represented objectively or rationally. "The greater portion will be intuitively perceived and sensed. That portion which can only be intuitively perceived and sensed goes back again into the continuum" of mind energy. This *irrational quantity triggers new experience* of physical and symbolic space and the cycle is repeated. Says Pereira:

> The irrational quantity, which is unfathomable, and which contains the "unknowable" essence, always unites the senses with a cosmological order, deepening the creative source in the mind, giving the experience of the continuum more reality.

The more one takes out of space, the greater the dimensions become. The more one takes away from the infinitudes as known quantities, the more one has left, because more is opened up. This is the irrational aspect of space. It is this irrational aspect of space which puts more depth into human experience.

The more space one is able to experience, the deeper the experience of space and the further the perceptions extend into space. In a cosmological continuum, the more one takes out of space, the more one puts back into space. The more one puts back into space, the deeper and greater the experience. This is the paradox of the dimensionality of space.[16]

8. Modern man, who "sees" only the rational, thereby cuts himself off from much of his own nature. A consciousness which envelopes the spiritual as well as the physical world *employs the powers of intuition in a never-ending probing into the mysteries of life.* The unknowns which we all sense have the ability to challenge our imagination; we approach each paradox as if it might be the golden link in the chain of knowledge. Each one tries to get hold of "the key which may unlock his secret hopes, his desires, his aspirations" and the quest for knowledge deepens. This is the springboard for "seeing the world for the first time, each time."

Inspired by his intuition from this deep spring of creative essence, man soars to the heights of exaltation in an ever-expanding endeavor to enlarge the small portion of space alloted to him as his share in creation. Man's spirit, stirred by the longings of his soul, continues its journey upward and onward—across the time-less span of vastness, searching for new horizons, for a glimmer of revelation, for a hope of immortality; ever-expecting to unite itself with God at the source, in the space of all creation.[17]

*Telescopic and spectroscopic observations, and increasingly exact
calculations, are transforming this comfortable spectacle of the universe into a vision that is very much more unsettling, one which
in all probability will profoundly affect our moral outlook and religious belief. . . when it has passed from the minds of a few initiates
into the mass consciousness of mankind as a whole. . . .*[1]

Teilhard de Chardin

6

A Philosophy of Space

It is inconceivable for most of us to imagine our earth as a comparatively tiny island in the universe from which, someday, large numbers of human beings will travel to distant places, unknown to us now except in a most general sort of way.

Humankind required eons to develop the ability to fly off the surface of the earth. Then, a half century later we had climbed up a few miles into the atmosphere in airplanes. Now, less than twenty years later, we have been to the moon and back.

In so doing, humankind has—even if unknowingly—embraced a destiny that is not earthbound. And this new capability will change us just as surely as the seafaring ships loaded with exotic cargoes changed sixteenth-century Europe. It would be a mistake, however, to suppose that the whole impact resides in our new technological prowess. That dimension is somewhat predictable; it can be assessed and even guided.

Beyond Earth

What may be even more significant than the space exploration equipment that we have invented, or the space technology by-products that are adding so much to modern medicine and other knowledge, or the new things we can do with the marvelous machines we can place in orbit around the earth—what may well be more fundamental than all of the visible impact, felt and yet to be felt, is what happened to the consciousness of humankind when we broke the chains of gravity and claimed "beyond earth" as human territory, too.

Lacking precise data, we can only speculate about the complete nature of the change. But, because we are talking about what we have experienced—about what we now perceive—we can have some confidence that this abstract map—a philosophy of space—corresponds to the terrain of reality.

Ancient and modern philosophy detail a variety of opinions about the birth of human consciousness. Apparently, at some dim distant time before recorded history, a primitive human mind looked into a pool of water, saw a face reflected there, and *knew for the first time* that he or she was the reflection. As Teilhard declares: "He not only knew, but he *knew* that he knew." That perception—seeing self and knowing it—represents possibly the biggest leap ever in human consciousness.

I believe that a similar enlargement of consciousness has occurred for a large proportion of the human population in the last ten years because of space exploration. The orbiting of manned spacecraft and unmanned satellites marked the beginning of a subtle process of "seeing new" that was culminated in the first *Apollo* flights to the moon and back.

Remember the awe, the pride, of seeing for the first time live on our home television screens—as the astronauts trained their cameras toward earth—that magnified brown-and-blue sphere—earth! And then the brilliant magazine pictures of that new image. That fuzzy, unreal representation of earth as an orbiting planet, first kindled by a schoolroom paper globe, suddenly flashed into focus. More than that, those pictures transported our eyes and spirits far out into space; for the first time we were conscious of *a whole earth!* *

Humanity—One Unit

Subsequent achievements in space have served to reinforce that image, nurturing the perception of humanity as one unit inhabiting one and the same home. More and more we see filtering into advertisements, popular literature, science-education units, and the like a picture of the *whole* planet earth. We find it increasingly easy to imagine ourselves on that planet, not as singular miniscule specks but as billions of lives linked together. A new paradox has been born: We are simultaneously as small, petty and inconsequential as a pinprick on that paper globe and a powerful Superhuman suddenly free of earth and racing triumphantly to the moon and beyond!

A new image of common humanity unceremoniously climbed aboard the crowded train of human consciousness. It whispers of a global unity that only makes us shrug our shoulders. After all, we have trouble even getting along with our relatives! It says all wars are *civil* wars, that people of every nation, rich and poor, are interdependent. It says that even though we cannot speak the same language, don't

---

* Breaking through the limits of old, limiting paradigms happens at many levels. For Dr. Gary Flandros of the University of Utah the limits were the givens of the orbits of the planets around the sun—each planet's orbit different. Accordingly it was believed that with current propulsion systems a trip to the outer planets by spacecraft would take up to thirty years. One night as he was contemplating the orbits of the planets, an idea occurred to him that had been outside the realm of hundreds of astronomers for centuries.

Following a hunch, Dr. Flandros calculated that once and only once every 175 years the planets *do* line up in such a way that a spacecraft can be sent around the solar system by bouncing it off the gravitational pull of Jupiter and Saturn. Such a trip would take only 8.9 years. The year of alignment is 1978. However, funding for the project was never authorized by Congress.

worship alike, and aspire to opposing goals, we all have our hands on the same rudder.

This is the era of an "international bicultural stretch" where we begin to struggle with acknowledging others' values and ways of living, begin to invest energy in finding the means of getting along, even though we are different. Up to now, at least, the West has had all the advantages. Seeing what others lack, we hurt only at the moral or intellectual level. When those who lack perceive that they are linked to those who have, the hurt is the horror of disease, hunger, hatred, envy.

We are only starting to grasp these details. For the moment we can only handle the long-distance lens. Earth is a huge spaceship circling a giant star, an immense hydrogen-powered furnace of heat, light, and other energy that will last approximately 12 billion more years. Together with the other planets, earth and our moon traverse the Milky Way Galaxy every quarter of a billion years, flying in formation at 60,000 miles per hour around the sun.

What will be the result of this new awareness? No one has the slightest idea. It will have to suffice for now that we know we have passed into a new beginning.

New Vistas

Accompanying the vision of a whole earth are several other subtle psychological dividends of moving into space, stepping onto the moon, and landing automated equipment on Mars. I alluded earlier to the obvious fact that space travel has opened up vast new territories for humankind. How exciting that is to the human spirit. For the first time in 400 years, we have been able to plan on going new places. The energy and enthusiasm that accompanies opening up new frontiers easily invades every other dimension of human life.

Exploration has a spiritual quality, writes Mircea Eliade

in *Cosmos and History.* He likens the settlement of an uncultivated country to an act of creation. Occupying a new place is a symbolic repetition, albeit on a small scale, of the transformation of chaos into cosmos by the Divine act of creation. Thus, "the ritual of taking possession is only a copy of the primordial act of the creation of the world," he argues.[2]

In struggling to prevail, man, with his science and technology, has embarked upon a whole new era of creation, characterized by his leaving earth. *In this sense, the human adventure is only beginning.* Up to now, man has been restricted in developing his creative powers because he was overwhelmed by toil. His technology has set him increasingly free, so that he is now free to be as human—and as creative—as he wishes to be. And I believe there is no limit to his creative ability or to his deep-seated need to be creative. He found out how to make fire when the only source of heat he knew was the sun, to sail an uncrossed sea when a route by land was already known, to conquer a continent because he could not see the end of it. Now space must be explored, the solar system traversed.

Moon Landing a Symbol

Neil Armstrong's "small step" down the ladder of the moon lander was the symbolic opening up of the virgin territory of the moon for the "giant step" of all humankind. That creative act, claiming the moon for all nations, was transcendent; humankind at last had a physical place that did not belong to anyone but belonged to all. Now, at least symbolically, there was a place where the human will could roam unfettered by previous failures, guilt, and selfishness.

This symbolic new territory was soon joined by new abstract territories of measurement and awareness as more and more sophisticated satellites were placed into orbit around the earth. So the machines of modern science opened new spheres of knowledge: radiation belts around the planet, weather patterns, mineral and agricultural resources. Communication satellites poised above the earth then linked all of the old, seemingly separate earth territories into one instantaneous electronic territory. A war halfway around the world now can unfold impartially each night on the six o'clock news. Here, again, is incalculable potential for changed human lives.

Moving into space also speaks to the need in humankind to be freed from all of the "old business" of life: immediate surroundings, limiting environment, unfathomable cycles of human misery. One of the ironies of the times is that it is easier for us to go to the moon than to wipe out a slum, easier to operate by radio signals a soil analyzer on Mars than to clean up polluted skies, easier to weld hundreds of different industries and thousands of their workers together in a vast technological enterprise than to forge brotherhood in one single neighborhood.

Earth and Sky

The earth is where we are rooted. It is the solid mass that allows us to stand upright. It offers us the security of gravity which we feel will never, ever fail us. Likewise, the sky is part of our homeland, an aesthetic vault that encloses the place where we live. It encompasses all sides of the measured horizon of our lives. Together the earth and the sky comprise the place we are assigned: our home, our cradle.

The earth, then, is the element of support. The sky is the element of containment, or of extension, which allows us to move. We, as human beings, are both "set" on the earth and "set free" in the sky. In the sky we are given the possibility of moving out into the infinite universe. Yet, it is only because we are rooted that we can even grasp the dimensions of the possible that lie beyond mother earth.

It is true that we are exaggerating when we pretentiously boast that we have conquered space. In the face of astronomical distances this simply is not true. But the symbolic meaning is immense. The physical transcendence that was encapsuled both symbolically and in fact, when humankind was propelled beyond earth's atmosphere, may well have been a grand watershed in human history. Until that moment the whole of human experience was rooted in the constant of being bound to earth. One could never escape earth; even an airplane could never fly so high as to wriggle out of the untiring grasp of gravity.

A Transcendence

But then suddenly the miracle happened. Mankind cracked the vault that sealed the boundary of life. The tie to the earth was loosed. We were set free into the infinite universe. There was and is no shield. No support. No landmarks. No ordinates. No center, up or down. No right or left. There was and is only the unfathomable depth of cosmic space—nothing but a limitless sky.

Religious men and women may choose to try to ignore the nuances of this transcendence, but the human spirit has found the open door. We may live in relationship with God, believing the old limits properly define the sphere of the Church, or we may live in relationship with God believing that creation and our calling to share in creation reach out to the future in all directions. The difference? Perhaps it is nothing; perhaps it is everything.

At least three other meanings, more speculative and difficult for us to conceptualize, may be seen in the wake of our venture into outer space. They are generally based on the as yet shaky assumption that travel to the other planets and beyond will become routine and available to large segments of the world population.

One is that colonizing outer space may be necessary in order to continue the human family. If at some time in the distant future, life became untenable on this planet, exporting civilization to other planets might be the supremely human act: saving mankind from extinction.

A second possibility is that we will treat the planets as scientific laboratories, setting off certain causal chains of biological processes, instigating a new family of humanity in a new time. We would become the authors or organizers of part of the universe beyond earth.

The third meaning occurs as space travelers return to earth, and as they regard this planet as the homeland of mankind. As the starting point for space journeys, "mother" earth would be viewed with tenderness and affection. A quality of unity that makes it possible to sponsor interplanetary travel would be highly valued; attention would be focused on cosmic problems, rallying the many different races and cultures on earth in cooperation and mutual ventures.

And so these are the ingredients of a philosophy of space, a mixture of the familiar and the bizarre. In part, they suggest that we are changed at the core. The picture is of an expanded psyche, a consciousness that is ranging past earth into the cosmos, a spirit that has been lifted from the mountaintops to the stars. Standing now at the boundary between the age of gravity and the infinity of space, we ponder celestial as well as earthly purpose. What does God wish of us now?

My response is that we must be open to the future. Indeed, I believe that: "Compared to the wondrous years ahead, all our recorded history with its magnificent procession of saints, seers, poets, philosophers, lawgivers, and light-givers, all the mighty dead and the billions of humble dead—all these will seem only a prologue to a drama beyond even the dreams of mankind's ancient gods." [3]

Instead of taking men's freedom from them, thou didst make it greater than ever. Didst thou forget that man prefers peace, even death, to freedom of choice in the knowledge of good and evil? Nothing is more seductive for man than his freedom of conscience, but nothing is a greater cause of suffering. And behold, instead of giving a firm foundation for setting the conscience of man at rest forever, thou didst choose what was utterly beyond the strength of men, acting as though thou didst not love them at all—(thou who didst come to give thy life for them). Instead of taking possession of men's freedom thou didst increase it and burdened the spiritual kingdom of mankind with its sufferings forever. [Lindaman's emphasis] *Thou didst desire man's free love, that he should follow thee freely, enticed and taken captive by thee. In place of the rigid ancient law, man must hereafter with free heart decide for himself what is good and what is evil, having only Thy image before him as a guide.*

Dostoevski

Not until a man is finished with the future can he be entirely and undividedly in the present. . . . But only by conquering it, is one finished with the future, and faith does exactly this, for its expectation is victory.

Kierkegaard

7

"The Evidence of Things Not Seen"

Visitors to my office often notice an oil painting on the wall and comment how striking it is. What is especially intriguing to them is the juxtaposition of images not usually associated together. Dominating the picture is the figure of the man Christ. In his left hand, outstretched with palm open and upturned, is a tiny space-suited astronaut. His hands are raised in praise and adoration as he looks up into the face of Christ. A shaft of radiant light links their faces. Christ's right arm also is outstretched and appears to be beckoning the astronaut on into the universe. In the background are representations of the planets.

When viewing the painting, one's first thought is the obvious: Man, represented by the astronaut, is in the hand of God and responds in love and worship. And, upon reflection, other ideas surface: Christ's *lordship* is strongly stated; he is God of man on earth, man in space; God of the earth, God of the heavens. Second, this is a God who beckons man toward *growth, learning, exploration.* The Author of Creation—by means of the lives of every human being—continues the creation dynamic. Third, the astronaut symbolizes new achievement, for mankind has with this bold stroke demonstrated innumerable *new capabilities* of seeing and acting in the universe. There is affirmation here of hope.

Hope . . .

Deep in our bones, ingrained at the center of the human spirit, no matter how poor or hungry and hurt we are,

107

we all anticipate, expect, and hope for a better tomorrow. Christian and non-Christian, believers and non-believers, we all are animated by faith. We are explorers, and we have come to understand that there is no qualitative difference between pioneers forging Western rivers for the first time and landing the first astronauts on the moon. The "moving-out" characteristic is constant throughout nature. A grub is snug in its cocoon, but when the appointed time comes it breaks out, flexes new butterfly wings, and flutters away to somewhere it has never been. It does not know why but something commands it just as something commands salmon to swim thousands of miles to spawn. And a child does not lie motionless in its cradle; in wiggling and turning, the infant begins the lifelong process of reaching out toward unseen horizons.

Yes, we have to admit that this beautiful spirit can be squashed, that people and events can stifle the burning light of faith in the human heart. This is a fact of our world we must not overlook. But, on the other hand, we need not be obsessed by the negative. We have everything to gain as we ally ourselves with the positive: There are so many possibilities; there is so much hope, growth, vision and sharing, so much that we can accomplish.

A Mid-course Correction

If we may borrow an image from the space era, we might see the present age as the optimum moment in history for humankind to make a decisive *mid-course correction*. Now is the time to decide to steer the ship of humanity toward affirmation or negation, toward adventure or retreat, toward hope or fear. The beauty of a mid-course correction is that it may well reside in the tiny miracles of any number of people; *a relatively minor change in our direction now may, a hundred years hence, mean the difference between life and nonlife on this planet.* Today does seem to be the "time between" that Ray Bradbury, the prophetic science fiction writer, and others have described.

Teetering on the brink of life and death in this "time between," we yearn for release from the failures that litter the present tense. Some, frustrated by the chaos and blinded by despair, lash out at their fellows; others withdraw. Some, though not ignoring these troubles, are busy searching out the good and cultivating it for the precious commodity it is. We are asking what God is saying to us now. We admit the complex dynamics of the present age are frustrating and even painful, and yet we are thrilled to be actively involved in the unlocking of both age-old and spanking new mysteries of life.

New Understanding

Four hundred years ago some people were asking, "What causes night and day?" Many people thought that was a silly question and wanted to have nothing to do with it. But some persisted, and in time they learned the answer. As a result, an entirely new understanding of the universe began to emerge. Eventually, we came to regard our planet with new eyes; we saw our role change from conqueror and user to steward. We came to blame God for less and less as superstition diminished and knowledge accumulated. We became more fully human as we began to wear the awesome yoke of responsibility—both personal and corporate. We caught a glimpse of the wholeness of nature, and we knew that even the starving peasant halfway around the earth from us was a brother. We accepted our role as builders, as creators of a new world.

The process feeds itself. Moved by faith, we embrace the future.

In this great human effort of creating and giving birth to a new, shared future, of *consciously directing history, we discover our own self and we discover each other.* [Lindaman's Italics]

We discover our self and our own identity to the degree that we become actively involved in creating our own future, in being subjects rather than objects of history. We affirm our personal identity as unique and as human to the degree that we no longer need to conform to external determinants to shape our identity, i.e., we no longer need to define ourselves by national, racial or other external determinants because we have grown beyond these constraining labels on self.

Ultimately, we become actualized as persons not because we seek actualization, but because we act on behalf of and in response to something which is greater than self. In the act of creating a more human future, we discover and become self.[1]

So the seemingly silly questions may not be silly at all. In asking "What is night and day?" or "What is the moon?" or "What is energy?" we are planting seeds that alter our relationship with the universe. Everything changes: our consciousness, our values, our ethics, and our sense of self.

The Phenomena of Mystery

Yet, we must still clean out our mental closets; some of the old clothes of the past may retard or deform our new growth. For example, one of the unfortunate casualties of the headlong rush of science in our technological age—with the emphasis upon a mechanical, factual approach to problem-solving—has been a general devaluation of the phenomena of "mystery." As science whittled away one superstition after another, a careless overgeneralization took root which grandly asserts that good science excludes mystery, that anyone with a logical, practical mind acts solely on the basis of "the sure thing."

That mental image of science at the opposite pole of mystery, of knowledge being contrary to religion, must be challenged. One who has been influential in debunking this myth is E. F. Schumacher, author of the international best-seller, *Small Is Beautiful.* Writing in *Resurgence,* an undated Journal of the Fourth World, Schumacher notes that matters of mystery should not be associated solely with religion. He laments the decline of the remarkable paradoxical marriage of mystery and science which inspired so much of the technological and information revolution. The "science of mystery," the pursuit of knowledge of the things we cannot understand, best serves the human condition, he says, when it ranges well beyond religion to permeate one's whole life. The degree to which mystery, this open-ended approach, is operative in our lives may well determine *"the extent to which we can acquire the knowledge of non-knowledge, the tolerance of non-knowledge, the certainty of certain things that cannot be known."* [Lindaman's Italics]

To the credit of the Christian faith, knowledge and mystery are integral elements. The Christian is not called to mindless, blind belief in ghosts and angels but to the person of a historical Christ who spanned the chasm between the finite and the infinite, the known and the unknowable.

God's Creation

Pierre Teilhard de Chardin once described the universe as a "seamless robe." We are part of that robe—the atoms of carbon, oxygen, nitrogen, and hydrogen, the atoms in our bodies—were literally cooked in a giant star ages ago. These atoms are no different from the atoms in the stars right now. I cannot help but think of myself as part of the greatness of creation. And when I look at the earth, as I now can from the moon and outer space, I see earth as God's creation. And once I confess to myself that *this is God's creation,* not a chance combination of atoms in a cosmic test tube, I have a new idea of myself. *I too have been created.* My Creator must know me better than I know myself. Therefore it is not just the righteousness of overt deeds that counts, which I can control with my will. But if he knows me better than I know myself because I am "of him," then what really counts is *purity of purpose.* I have, you see, gone from a space-age view of the earth to me, as a child of God.

God's Redemption

The apostle Paul wrote, "Through him God chose to reconcile the whole *universe* to himself, making peace through the shedding of his blood upon the cross—to reconcile all things through him alone" (Col. 1:20, NEB). Amazing, the whole universe! The historical Christ is the cosmic Christ of the universe. And we talk of humanity as being of the same substance as the universe, having in addition consciousness. Paul also witnessed to the personal Christ: God revealing to the world "the riches of the glory of this mystery, which is Christ in you, the hope of glory" (Col. 1:27, RSV). We are not a fungus on a galactic slag heap; we are children of God.

Perhaps the most unique dimension of Christianity is its personal quality. God has revealed himself in actual fact as "Somebody" and "Something" for humankind—not as a distant absolute, not as a pure "Thou." The Somebody is Christ; the Something is his lordship, his love for each one of us. He is personal to me; he reaches me. He touches me to the extent that I let him empower me to join in the ongoing, unfolding creation. As Bonhoeffer put it, "God became man in order that man might become man"—might have this incredible link of consciousness with God, might receive word again and again from the dimension of the eternal, the infinite. Christ, the unique revelation of God on earth, speaks to everyone who has human consciousness. To be fully human, we are open to this special dimension—the ultimate, infinitely significant.

Looking back over time, the biggest single event that occurred on this small planet is that Christ died on a cross. In some way or other, the fate of every human being is bound up in that event. It is clear that what we believe or do not believe about the crucifixion/resurrection event has a profound impact upon the meaning we derive from existence. This event seems to hold the key to an understanding of what life is meant to be.

The Role of Faith

My faith in Christ, as I perceive it and experience it, is not a mere section out of my life. Rather, my faith is an impulse that cuts across it. Its purpose is not so much to *add* something *else* to my life, but to *unify* and *guide* my existence. It provides me with a sense of how I am related to what I do, to others, to the world. The gospel is, I believe, a strong document on social unity. God did not create us for life in isolation. Christ's life, which illustrates what man is meant to be, was ministering to people's deepest needs—physical *and* spiritual. I believe it is God's will that those men and women who have chosen to follow Christ should work together to affirm and develop the dignity that is the birthright of every person. That means involving ourselves in the political, yes, and the social and the economic orders so that the God in every person is nurtured and given expression.

The word "joy" describes the social phenomenon of Christianity. Paul Tillich says that, "Joy is possible only when we are driven towards things and persons—because of what they are—and not because of what we can get from them." Joy is the surprise of fellowship. Creation is moved toward God's will through our relationships.

Faith in Christ, for me, has been the discovery of the surpassing significance of life, as I believe it to be empowered by him, to build a world of hope, love, justice, freedom and freedom from want—today. Each life is either a message of this hope, or a potential expression of it. The decision is always up to us. The proclamation of the Word ever puts that decision before us. That is why we need to hear the Word over and over again. Said Bultmann, "Every moment in time bears within it the unborn secret of revelation, and every moment can thus be qualified but you must awaken it." Revelation, discovering what God intends for my life, is a continuing activity. And while we cannot ever say of God totally what he objectively is, we do have the knowledge of what effect he has on our lives. To test whether or not revelation is real, we can ask this question: How do I want to see the essence of my life— as my establishing or winning my life and my authenticity by my own resources, my own reason, my own action, *or* by the grace of God which is in Christ?

What if we doubt? How can we be sure enough to take action without being blindly fanatical?

Doubt = Growth

One of the most important discoveries of my adulthood is the role that doubt plays in growth. Someone once said that doubt is the "permanent horizon of faith," meaning that doubts keep us open to new truths, beckoning us to ask new questions and to invest new energy in searching for answers. If we knew something for certain, there would be no need of faith. Doubt keeps us involved:

> You are never dedicated to something you have complete confidence in. No one is fanatically shouting that the sun is going to rise tomorrow. They know it is going to rise. When people are fanatically dedicated to political or religious faiths, or any other kind of dogmas or goals—it is always because these dogmas or goals are in doubt. . . .[2]

We should not be fearful of doubts; they are allies, friends, that open us up to new possibilities in faith. However, we should take seriously the apparent relationship between fanatic behavior and insecurity; the more fanatic we become, perhaps the more unsure we are. Dogmatic behavior may reflect a weakening faith that needs to be opened up by hope.

We must live with the reality of our finite nature. We can recognize history only after it is made. We can only see the modifications of our spirit after the fact. But God, on the other hand, looks ahead. And this is the heart of the meaning of faith: we can participate in divine providence—the future of God. God's future, tomorrow, a thousand years from today. We participate as we refuse to accept the future as merely a fateful repetition of the worst of the past.

The Resurrection Hope

The resurrection hope of Christians leads us to expend ourselves to continually grasp new possibilities from the expected future. This is why the cross is the symbol of the hope of the earth. The possibilities are unlimited; the future is not fixed. We are participants in creation. Time, by itself, as it passes by, does not bring the future—we are the agents of the future. Writes Teilhard de Chardin, "Christ guides time to his day through us." To believe that is to participate in the future of God.

This is how I see Christian faith: Through the history of Christ and the promises of the gospels, God reveals his future to humankind. It is through Christ's resurrection and through hope aroused (the resurrection in me) that God exerts an influence in the present and on the future.

Holding to that central belief, we then are free to place our own image of the future in the context of a future—for me and for all humanity—that is God's.

Man has now become conscious of having come into the full possession of his sphere of action. Having reached this apogee of responsibility and freedom, holding in his hands all of his past, and all of his future, he will make the choice between arrogant autonomy and loving excentration.[1]

Teilhard de Chardin

Man is a duality of mysterious grandeur and pompous aridity. A vision of God and a mountain of dust. It is because of his being dust that his iniquities may be forgiven . . . and it is because of his being an image . . . that his righteousness is expected.[2]

Abraham Heschel

8
The Logic of Being Human

Americans like to think we are a nation of strong values. We are rightfully proud of the founding documents of this country, for they set forth an ambitious and farseeing set of societal principles and values. To our credit, we often transpose that same high-mindedness to our own personal values. So far, so good. Such is the stuff of building a brighter tomorrow.

Lesser Values

The trouble is, though, that a lesser quality of values functions at the operative level for most of us. The grand values are something of a smoke screen, a verbal "hype" that we employ to avoid carefully scrutinizing our acted-upon values. To a large degree, we are what we value. A selfish man values, in the final analysis, selfishness, no matter how loudly he proclaims his Christianity or his generosity.

With one hand we wave high the flag of democracy and with the other we are building a fence around our yards to keep out the "different" people in the neighborhood. We distrust "big government" and lobby strenuously for government aid in support of *our* pet projects. This double standard (the younger generation calls it hypocrisy) undoubtedly is a factor in the high incidence of suicide, divorce, crime, mental illness, and other personal and societal tragedies.

The incongruity of what we say and what we do is hardly

new, of course, but it is compounded by the revolutionary
changes in the past few decades. To be sure, we live in
a world that today hardly resembles that of twenty or thirty
years ago. Due to mass communications, almost anyone
in the Western world can now "see" more of the globe
in a few weeks than even the mightiest ruler a century
ago could view in a lifetime. Under these conditions, the
rigid local rules which formerly governed human behavior
have been vanishing like the morning's dew. We used to
feel confident in our smugness when we excused our behavior by alibiing "everybody is doing it." Everybody else
used to mean people down the road or even for several
miles around because that is as far as our consciousness
reached. Today, we can only feel uncomfortable with the
lie of "everybody else."

Values Transmission

Meanwhile, we have moved into an era of changing the
means of values transmission. From earliest times through
our own pioneer past, values were formally and informally
passed down from grandparents to grandchildren; multiple
generations lived together, and the elderly cared for the
young while the mothers and fathers did the harvesting
and hunting. Then, almost overnight, the family shrunk
to the skeleton of just parents and children. The elderly
were shunted off to rest homes and retirement centers;
value transmission was up to Mom and Dad.

That was hardly a smart thing to do. Dad was busy at
the office and came home in no mood to sit down and
play with the children. And Mom—deprived of immediate
access to the servants that used to help with dinner, do
the dishes, wash and iron, and occupy the children—was
getting a severe case of cabin fever; she was depressed,
lonely, frightened, resentful. If she didn't turn on the TV
to keep the kids quiet she plopped them in a day-care

center and went to work for someone who paid her money for her work. The result: today a high percentage of the young have been abandoned to the television set, the streets, and the schools.

At both levels—societal and personal—who is to see that the fundamental tenets are passed on to the young?

The Irony of It All

Just when *Homo sapiens* acquires the capacity to create the world as he sees fit, at the point in history when for the first time the whole world is interrelated by economics, energy, food, travel, and communications, we suddenly find that we are cut off from in-depth personal relationships with peers and older and younger generations. We barely know other families living on the same block. Ironically, this happens just as we are realizing that

> . . . we are unalterably bound together. We share a common dependency on one earth system. We stand together in relationship with one air, water, land and life-support system. We have the same needs, the same potentialities, the same capacities for participating in destruction or for participating in creation. We share a common possibility for annihilation or fulfillment. We no longer have many diverse and isolated histories. Our cultural and national histories have converged in one commonly shared present and future reality.[3]

The good in this is that, accompanying the sense of wholeness and interrelatedness, is a growing understanding that we are part of the transformation process.* Our

---

* Erich Fromm, writing in *To Have or to Be,* his 1976 book surveying the human condition, found special significance in the increase in numbers of people who place priority on quality of life over quantities of possessions and things consumed: "My personal estimate is that the young people (and some older ones) who are seriously concerned with changing from the having to the being mode number more than a few dispersed individuals. I believe that quite a large number of groups

powers of awareness have been expanded: we are observing with some objectivity what we are doing to our world and to each other, foreseeing what will happen and what could happen, and sensing the tremendous responsibility we have in guiding this maturation process.

Publication in 1977 of *Taking Charge*, a paperback collection of practical suggestions for evolving a more responsible life-style (which was prepared by the *"Simple Living Collective"* of the American Friends Service Committee in San Francisco), may represent a landmark in the development of new values for this nation. The authors approach the knotty question of production/consumption most realistically; they have assembled a practical, understandable guide to simple living as it relates to work, politics, clothing, health, energy, food, community, personal growth, and the world as a whole. The call is to turn away from the mania of acquisitiveness, where people "become objects whose main purpose is to consume whatever is offered them"—toward simple living: "consciously returning material things to their proper role, as the means and tools by which human ends may be achieved and human creativity fostered."

What is simple living? What are the new values we should consider? *Taking Charge* is specific; simple living includes:

"An emphasis on replacing wasteful consumption with creativity and usefulness wherever possible.

"The use of energy, natural resources, and technology as means for facilitating human growth, self-reliance,

---

and individuals are moving in the direction of being, that they represent a new trend transcending the having orientation of the majority, and that they are of historical significance. It will not be the first time in history that a minority indicates the course that historical development will take. The existence of this minority gives hope for the general change in attitude from having to being. . . . " [4]

mastery of skills, and sharing, rather than as ends in themselves.

"The redistribution of resources and restructuring of institutions so that everyone's basic needs are met before luxury items are produced which benefit only a few.

"Working to end production that threatens human life or makes it less enjoyable. This includes noninformative advertising, arms production, and planned obsolescence.

"Recognition that material goods are the basis for human existence, not the source of abundance. Real abundance is found in human creativity, and richness in personal relationships, culture, and the human spirit." [5]

Teach/Transmit/Apply

Clearly, one of the most critical and urgent questions we must resolve has to do with values and how we plan to teach/transmit/apply them. We have hardly begun to examine whether the values and assumptions which served well enough thus far in our nation's history will suffice to guide our nation in the next century, or to foster a larger, workable global community. As we move into the next century, we will experience worldwide shortages of vital commodities, ranging from the age-old problem of too little food to the newer problems of diminishing supplies of fuel and metals. Will the kind of hostility and exploitation that marked the past—where the strong get stronger and the weak get weaker—continue unabated? Will our heightened consciousness of our interrelatedness be translated, by us, into norms of mutual respect, equity, and cooperation among even diverse groups?

We have little evidence before us that gives us confidence that the old values, even if they were transmitted unbroken to our children, would build a heterogeneous functional consensus.

It seems to me that the burden of "unity through diversity" falls especially hard upon education and persuasive communication. The traditional methods of establishing cooperation—hierarchies, legislation, coercion—rely heavily upon eliminating differences among people. But the human spirit refuses to be squelched: Arabs cling to their ways and Jews to theirs. Irish Catholics and Irish Protestants are unyielding. Indians and blacks somehow retained a large degree of ethnic identity in the great "melting pot" of America.

Any hope of meaningful social change and large-scale cooperation must be built upon the reality of unyielding differences among the peoples of this earth. We must look to a global population comprised of widely differing, individual personalities and contrasting cultures who value, and therefore practice, living in concert with fellow inhabitants of this planetary home. Such a lofty goal requires, first of all, a healthy self-consciousness and self-worth that is not dependent upon winning at all cost. We must replace win/lose patterns with win/win strategies.

This is not simply a matter of snapping your fingers and, presto, life is different. One important reason why it is so difficult to escape the win/lose rut is that the whole thrust of production/consumption is quantitative. The person with *more,* or newer, or bigger, is perceived as the winner; the fellow with *less,* or the older, or the smaller, surely is the loser.

But as Erich Fromm rightly observes, "Consuming has ambiguous qualities: It relieves anxiety, because what one has cannot be taken away; but it also requires one to consume ever more, because consumption soon loses its satisfactory character. Modern consumers may identify themselves by the formula: *I am = what I have and what I consume.*" [6] What a tremendous burden this places on getting, taking, consuming, having; it does not nod in the least in the direction of relationships. But even seeing that others share this same obsession may be a vital beginning; it may open us to the importance of relating our personal values to the whole picture. And this sensitivity, once it has taken root, may be transferred to other perceptions.

People Need to Be Needed

We must begin to think of how each person may become aware of his or her role as an essential participant in both the immediate and extended world. People need to be needed, to feel significant, and this basic human quality can be a powerful magnet to draw diverse peoples together in shared tasks. Heschel, in discussing the essence of being human, says we have both a *bios* (life) dimension with the drives of food, sex, and power, and a dimension called *existence,* which embraces both *bios* and being human:

> Being human is a characteristic of a being who faces the question: *After satisfaction, what?* The circle of need and satisfaction, of desire and pleasure, is too narrow for the fullness of his existence. Bios, or life, requires satisfaction; existence requires appreciation. Satisfaction is a sensory experience bringing about an end to a desire. Appreciation is an imponderable experience, an opening up, the beginning of a thirst that knows no final satisfaction.
>
> From the perspective of a philosophy of satisfaction, the quest for significant being, which assumes that complete satisfaction is not desirable or conceivable or even possible, must be regarded as a perversion. Yet the logic of being human insists that man's total existence is pledged to the truth that the quest for significant being is the heart of existence.
>
> We do not crave that quest; we find ourselves involved in it. There is no planning, no initiative on our part to embark upon it. There are only moments of finding ourselves in it.

Animals are content when their needs are satisfied; man insists not only on being satisfied but also on being able to satisfy, on being a need, not simply on having needs. Personal needs come and go, but one anxiety remains: Am I needed? There is no human being who has not been moved by that anxiety.

It is a most significant fact that man is not sufficient to himself, that life is not meaningful to him unless it is serving an end beyond itself, unless it is of value to someone else.[7]

This is the way the universe is made. It is the way Christ demonstrated, and it is the way creation can be joined with the amazing ingenuity of man. We can choose to ignore this reality or we can meet it and employ it to our corporate advantage. We can persist in trying to level differences, invest in power plays, in conflict, *or we can accept differences along with what we have in common* and pool our resources to move toward harmony and purposeful lives for all.

Possibilities and Limitations

The person of the future is called to be a sober, realistic assessor of both the possibilities and the limitations of individual and group activity. Human institutions may express God's continuing activity of creation and, at the same time, imprison the human spirit in the muck of rhetoric, rules, and busyness. Institutions tend to be self-serving and ultimately idolatrous. In our servant role we are called to advocate for fairness and equity, taking care that neither we nor others are shunted aside for the sake of bureaucratic efficiency or shortsightedness. We should not put all of our cooperativeness eggs in the basket of temporal institutions such as government, *for institutions can never deliver human fulfillment or ultimate meaning.* When they presume to do so, they are tyrannical. It is the role of the "future thinker," guided by the Christian imperative, to help society *distinguish between justice in the temporal sense and fulfillment in the ultimate sense.*

We must reserve energy and resources for inventing new channels of action, for working outside of the old order, for keeping alive our private dreams. Both, working in the system and outside of it, are needed. We must have both kinds of creative pressure.

Our founding fathers did not presume that this new nation would redeem humanity. They fully expected that human nature would continue much as they found it, so they provided a constitution that would protect the people against tyranny. How did they do this?

- They dared to believe that the intentional fashioning of a political society was within the capacity of human beings.
- They dared to build upon the shared values of the people of the colonies.
- They dared to fashion a framework in which liberty and justice for all might be pursued.
- And they dared to do all of this without promising an instant realization of those ideals.

In short, *they assumed a continuous, participatory revolution!* Reinhold Niebuhr once put it in these words: "Man's capacity for justice makes democracy possible, but man's inclination to injustice makes democracy necessary."

Ethic and Ethos

I make these comments about values with conviction, but I do not want to have my concern for values, purpose, and meaning seen primarily in terms of a relationship to religion. In the church, or academia or business, in a secular or nonsecular world, there is urgent need for both an ethic and an *ethos* out of which responsible, effective, and constructive lives can be lived. A society that has lost its way with respect to fundamental values is likely to be in trouble in all directions. Corruption in government usually means corruption in business, and vice versa. And an educational system that ignores or downgrades the issues of values definition, discovery, and affirmation is failing government, business, and all other elements in society.

What we need today is a common frame of reference to use in comprehending once again where we have been and where we might go. We are indebted to Geoffrey Vickers for a concise and eloquent summary of the past tense:

> Looking back over history, the rational mind of the eighteenth century declared the human condition to be a triple slavery and promised it a triple emancipation. Men were enslaved by economic want, by political domination and by religious superstition. Trade and technology would free them from the first, democratic institutions from the second and science from the third. Freed from tyranny by nature, men and gods, free men, it was assumed, would need no more regulation than human reason would supply.
>
> The great emancipation has done its work and posed its own problems. In each of its three areas, freedom, having dissolved one order, has left another to be created. The new productive powers create intolerable inequalities between man and man, nation and nation, present and future. They waste resources, pollute the environment and multiply populations so as to defeat even their own productivity. The dissolution of a power structure legitimized by custom leaves authority too weak for its new and mounting tasks, makes room for other powers which in their turn need to be controlled, and calls for new authorities which need to be created. The dissolution of religious authority leaves a void which is only partly filled by new and warring ideologies.[8]

What we thought we had solved, we hadn't solved at all! These three "failures of history"—economic, political and religious—could well be the tasks again of the next hundred years:

> These must be, economically, to conserve the planet's resources and to distribute its product acceptably between man and man, nation and nation, present and future. Politically, they will be not merely to control but to organize and legitimize the huge concentrations of power which will be needed, not only in government but in all the major institutions of society. Ideologically and psychologically the task will be to develop and spread an appreciation of the human situation and an acceptance of its inherent obligations such as will make the other two tasks possible. These are tasks to excite a liberal mind. They may be possible but they are none the less inspiring.[9]

Christian Values

I believe we are fortunate in finding in Christianity values that combine the dignity of the individual and compassion for the poor and oppressed. We need a vigorous sense of self-worth and individuality that fuels our private goals and strategies to do the impossible, and we require the sensitivity and caring that keep us from running over those who "get in the way" or from ignoring those who do not get in the way. These twin characteristics are not found, to my knowledge, in any other religion. The gospel reveals a God who values us so much personally, as individual and unique persons, that his spirit is in us. Little old fallible me is linked directly to the infinite God. I am something special! You are, too!

The gospel also calls us to be Christ's recruits in human liberation: Luke 4:18–19 says, "The Spirit of the Lord is upon me, because he has anointed me to preach good news to the poor. He has sent me to proclaim release to the captives and recovering of sight to the blind, to set at liberty those who are oppressed, to proclaim the acceptable year of the Lord" (RSV).

Christianity, beyond the ceremonial systems and ecclesiastical hierarchies, is a declaration of universal dignity for humankind. "It encourages a way of life in which *leaders are servants* (Mark 10:45) and in which the way to be fully a child of God is to *be a peacemaker* (Matthew 5:9)." [10]

The task is immense. Yet, if we center our values on the vision of personal dignity and compassion, we will progress in the solution of the sea of human problems. We are able always to employ the power of Christian faith and hope. To paraphrase Jurgen Moltmann: "For the believer the *saving future of God* appears over the misery of the world's sin and evil . . . in the resurrection of Christ."

For man's story, in brief, is essentially that of a creature who has abandoned instinct and replaced it with cultural tradition and the hard-won increments of contemplative thought. The lessons of the past have been found to be a reasonably secure instruction for proceeding against the unknown future.[1]

Loren Eisely

Then the Lord answered Job out of the whirlwind: Who is this that darkens counsel by words without knowledge? Gird up your loins like a man, I will question you. . . . Where were you when I laid the foundation of the earth? Tell me if you have understanding.

Job 38:1–4

9
"Being Called Upon to Answer"

The world of science since 1930 has shown us that today we can see only one millionth of the total physical reality that lies within the full range of the electromagnetic spectrum. We used to think reality was limited only to what we could see with our eyes, hear with our ears, or could taste or touch. But we cannot see X rays, infrared rays, cosmic rays, and we cannot see atoms in motion. We cannot see the stars move—though they move a thousand times faster than a rocket to the moon.

A Changing Universe

We also have discovered in recent years that the universe, too, is changing. Astronomers have learned that a million solar systems are being added to the universe *every hour.* The old picture of a static universe has been replaced by one of a dynamic universe filled with evolving cosmic objects. Everything is changing; stars appear, grow and die; clouds of gas and dust and galaxies develop; everything is in motion.

There is more here than we thought!

Exploration into the secrets of God's universe, from the innermost nuclei to the outermost nebulae, is eliminating much misinformation, while at the same time implementing an ability to apprehend information from all around our planet in split seconds, and giving us a vivid new awareness of other humans and other possibilities here on earth and beyond this planet. This is something never before experienced by humanity.

Old Patterns Going

The old patterns of accepting whatever life hands you have begun to disappear. We are just too conscious of how everything is changing and how much we do impact change to cling to the old notions that inhibited the creative impulse. Barbara Ward describes how our former image of reality held us in a predominantly passive role:

> . . . the whole creation was drawn in to confirm and illustrate a profound and conservative bias against innovation and unpredictable change. Man's *cycle* of life from birth to death, the *return* of the seasons, stars *wheeling* in the firmament, the *passage* of the years, all pointed to a *revolving* reality perpetually renewing the *same* patterns. Thus they demanded from man, as the highest wisdom, the mood of acceptance and resignation. . . .[2]

Quite naturally, that posture was reinforced in nearly everything people did; it is reflected in architecture, art, education, religion, politics, commerce, taboos, and myths. Our world is geared to order, recurrence, conformity— or so we thought. In reality, our world is energy, flux, innovation, interrelatedness, exceptions, and paradoxes.

Societal systems previously embraced totally the concept of determinism. The aim in life was to produce and acquire enough of the basic necessities to survive. Production capacity was a gear that generally was engaged by demand. The industrial age may be viewed in the context of mass production for a growing population consuming ever-increasing amounts of goods and services. And then, ever so subtly, the picture changed as social choices entered the fray. Once beyond necessities, we moved into the strange new realm of choosing among options. Where for thousands of years we were occupied with producing basic goods, we began to develop the skill of using and choosing.

Affluence, the promise and goal of twentieth-century America, came to be regarded in a different light once we had a good taste of it and weighed the results. We learned what it costs us in energy, in used-up resources, and in impact upon the human spirit. Affluence for what? More, more, more—clearly more was not the answer. And the gulf between what we enjoyed and what most of the rest of the world did not enjoy looms ever larger in our hearts.

Tougher Questions

The questions grew tougher and tougher: How should we employ an almost unlimited production capacity and capability? What should we produce for the highest good of all humankind? On what grounds and by whom are these choices made? Our nation's answers, to the degree that these questions were addressed, have been shaped almost entirely by political and economic considerations, not ethical, moral, or even Christian persuasions. Individually, some continue to wrestle with these questions. The meaning of life had become a particularly thorny dilemma.

We were stuck between opposing images. We could either see the world as containing forces to be managed, things to be used, or we could perceive the world in terms of forces and things to be understood and appreciated in the context of what they do to us as persons. But that was difficult to deal with, for the more we manipulated, the more we acquired and consumed, and the more entangled we became with activities that had nothing to do with our sense of meaning. The fog of materialism is thick with trivia that consumes energy and does little or nothing in the way of replenishing the spiritual stores.

We began to make some progress when we realized that not only was the universe, our world, and our awareness of the world changing; we were also changing. God did not conceive the good for man as a gift to be given to him in one complete package as a reward for good works or strong faith. No, man was left free to choose, free to err. God did not assemble us, wind us up, and set us ticking on a shelf. Not at all. From the embryo to the grave, from the first century to the twenty-first century, we are changing beings with our own destinies linked with all others who share our planet with us.

The Meaning of Living

The old questions about the meaning of life were usually answered philosophically in view of what the supposed nature of *being* was. Now, it seems to have evolved to a more complex and more promising focus: We are interested in the meaning of *living:*

> Living is a situation, the content of which is much richer than the concept of being. The term "human being" is apt to suggest that the human is but a mode of being in general, with the emphasis placed on being. Since the power of a term easily determines the image of what we undertake to explore, we must always keep in mind that it is the *living* man we seek to understand when we speak of the human being: human being as human living.
>
> Man's most important problems is not being but living. To live means to be at the crossroads. There are many forces and drives within the self. What direction to take? is a question we face again and again.
>
> Who am I? A mere chip from the block of being? *Am I not both the chisel and the marble?* Being and foreseeing? Being and bringing into being? [3]

Aha, here is the image of a person as both being and becoming, as both what is and unlimited possibilities! Yes, we were the brilliant tool-using animals that so dominated our perception of self over the past few centuries. But at the same time we were "mind-making, self-mastering, self-designing animals" whose dominant human trait is "the capacity for conscious, purposeful self-identification, self-transformation, and ultimately self-understanding. . . ." [4]

Participants in Creation

Man, too, is a participant in creation. We do not remain the same from the cradle to the grave, nor do we remain the same from the cave to the space capsule. There is no such entity as man in his final and permanent form. We can be more than we are. The present, says Moltmann, is the "advancing front line of time as directed purposefully towards its goal in the moving horizon of promise."

We are process, flex, and flux. We are always a breath away from being more than we are at the moment:

> To animals the world is what it is. But to man this world is in the making. To be human is to be on the way, striving, waiting, hoping; it means to intend, to decide, to challenge. Not merely to go on, to react, or to be an effect. It is to respond to wonder—*to put our wonder into the form of a question and then go out and answer the question.* It is to be discontent with just being around in the world. Being human is to be in a dilemma, it is to be cross-examined. Being human is being called upon to answer.[5]

I like to think of this quality as "the trust of human sacredness." We have been given a powerful gift that sets us apart from all the rest of creation. One of the burdens of this inestimable gift is an unquenchable thirst for meaning. This keeps us from being comfortable with achievement; it makes it impossible to endlessly run the treadmill of getting and using; it bumps us off the merry-go-round of ephemeral pleasures.

The pursuit of meaning does not guarantee that we shall ever conquer our problems or answer the questions. It does force us in the direction of being involved in the problems; it calls forth commitment. Warns Heschel, "It is self-deception to assume that man can ever be an innocent spectator. To be human is to be involved, *nolens volens,* to act and to react, to wonder and to respond. For man, to be is to play a part in a cosmic drama, knowingly or unknowingly." [6]

Gathering information is not enough. We must seek meaning actively by living boldly and with enthusiasm. I believe that meaning begins to enter our lives when we discover, by our actions, the surpassing significance of the "right now." Meaning is born when we discover that the world of creation is both a problem and a hope. And the context is always of a universe created by a transcendent God who in Christ "makes sense" out of all things. Each one of us is the work of God; we are not self-made or an accidental happening or biological combinations. God's purpose brings each person into being and rightfully places unique opportunities, possibilities, and even demands upon us.

With this understanding of creation, I realize more and more that my outward behavior, largely willed, is not all that matters. My creator does not view me by the appearance I make, does not perceive me as my acquaintances do. He knows me inwardly—even better than I know myself—and therefore what he asks of me is purity of purpose rather than righteousness of overt deed. In the example of Christ, I have been given a model for my use of the powers—good and bad—that are mine by virtue of my humanness.

A Quantum Jump

The ability to achieve the development of a meaningful existence on earth took a quantum jump when Jesus came to Peter with the basin and towel. We are told that Peter said, "Lord, you shall never wash my feet!" Peter was sure that the Lord of Life could *never* be a *servant*. After all, true power could never come that way! But Jesus replied, "If I do not wash you, you have no part in me." Jesus was saying it was necessary to acknowledge Him as a servant of man in order to participate in life with Him. Peter got the message, answering with zeal: "Not my feet only, but also my hands and my head!" (John 13:8–9, RSV).

The power to direct an army of wooden soldiers is in the hands of a young boy because the soldiers have no power to resist. The power needed to lead men and women is incomparatively greater because the ones that are led have powers of their own.

The Power of Servanthood

To think of God's power like that of the lad with the wooden soldiers degrades His power. True power in the world is of an entirely different sort. We saw it born in the servant role of Christ. We are invited to be servants of God in community with other believers. We need fellowship, for this is the arena of creation, the ground of creativity.

> The "community of faith" is that social reality where creativity is incarnated. It gains flesh and bones. In this community the future takes on space in the time still present: it is the "objectification of the Spirit," *the place where the creative insight and the creative intention become creative power.* [EBL's Italics]
> . . . .
> Insights in themselves are powerless. No matter how true, they are impotent to bring about change. Words and thoughts have no *ex opere operato* power. . . . In traditional theological language, the Word must become flesh: vision must become power if the world is to be redeemed. To the ethical question "What shall I do?"

the Bible replies by pointing to the community where
the logic of death and resurrection—or the logic of creativity—has assumed space and time and has determined
the style and direction of human interrelatedness. . . .
The question of the good is really the question of the
koinonia, the community which embodies the messianic
thrust of the creative intention.[7]

We have only been pointed in this direction; we know
virtually nothing about how to create the kind of community that opens up the future. Scripture leaves us short
of having any formula for duplicating community.

It acknowledges that the creative event erupts in history and assumes a social form, but it does not have
any formula for duplicating it. The community cannot
be mass-produced. We have no recipe for programing
its growth or proliferation. But then what are we to do?
The New Testament simply says: "Believe the good
news"—somewhere, somehow it is happening. "Re-
pent": throw away your old stethoscope and find a way
of hearing the heartbeat of the future already pulsating
in a community. And "be baptized": join it.[8]

God Makes New

Many, if not most of us, are timid. We feel out of place
in all but familiar circles. We prefer the known to the unknown, hold to the painfully familiar rather than reach
out to the hope or promise of the unfamiliar. We feel
lost when the dynamics are complex. However, we can
stack against this banality the gospel message and Christian
experience that "God makes new."

The heart of the Bible is that each one of us is God's
trustee for creation. As trustees, we are, in Christ, transformed into "new humanity." And, linked in fellowship,
we escape the bonds of weakness, fear, and failure. Com-

munity is a vehicle for drawing us into the future. As Alves eloquently sums up in *Tomorrow's Child,* "In the community of faith the form of human interrelatedness is not determined by the 'present evil world' but rather by the vision that has grown out of common longings and aspirations." [9]

We live through one of the great hours of history. The false gods are crumbling, and the hearts are hungry for the voice of God. But the voice has been stifled. To recapture the echo, we must be honest in our willingness to listen, we must be unprejudiced in our readiness to understand.[1]

Abraham Heschel

10
Doing More with Less

Surrounded, perhaps inundated, by the wondrous machines and objects which have been spewing forth from the gigantic belly of modern technology, and senses pounded incessantly by the tidal waves of competing signals, we struggle to discern what is flesh and what is plastic, what is the voice within, and what are messages from without.

Every now and then a head pokes out from the avalanche of things to survey the landscape; turning left and right, squinting into the bright lights of progress, eyes focused on the masked faces hurrying by for just a hint that others, too, are crying out for someone who cares, for someone who shares in bewilderment, and yet dedicatedly moves ahead in search of resolution and meaning.

Human Needs

How hard it is to remain sensitive to human needs, even one's own, when so many demands are made on our time—when there is so much to do, when there are so many choices to make. Humankind has never been especially adept at measuring up to the standards which conscience sets forth. But history is replete with genuine selfless attempts to divine and do good works. Intertwined with the drive to satisfy sensory appetite is an unswerving need to understand what life's purpose is.

Indeed, we cannot read accounts of the creation story and the many prophetic Old Testament commentaries about creation without seeing how man, from the beginning, has desperately sought to understand his origin. Now, of course, we are being challenged to understand both our *origin* and to plot the *course* that lies ahead.

Not too long ago there was practically no concern about participating in planning the future. In just the last two decades we have become aware that creation is present in future tense as well as past—that we are expected to play a part in it, and in ways we are still discovering, Christ will manifest himself in and through that which is yet to happen.

"And God saw everything that he had made, and, behold, it was very good" (Gen. 1:31). God not only created the world, but gave himself to it, and through Christ reconciles the world to himself. The world has worth. Nature, the universe, and technology are not adversaries. Man, made in the image of a creating God, is meant to tend, to explore, and to enjoy creation in all its complex ramifications. However, man's position is not that of an absolute sovereign, but that of a steward. He does not have the world at his disposal, but is made responsible for it.

New Levels of Responsibility

In examining the technological era, and what it portends, we are coming to know that there are new levels of responsibility ahead of man. Whole new qualities of possibility are yet to be developed. We also understand that our relationship with the world has been undergoing a massive and significant change. The changes began with the deliberate making of fire, moved to cultivation of plants, the domestication of animals, the settlement of villages, and then on to cities. Then came the harnessing of power other than muscles, and in the blink of history we awoke in the midst of a technological age with its nuclear and electronic know-how. Now we have reached the point where we can no longer react naturally to our surroundings because, for the most part, our environment is artificial.

To react naturally to a largely man-made environment would be disastrous. Yet, we are still plagued with a strong tendency to live with the false idea that we can, and that everything will automatically work out all right. We still view technology as a giant hardware store where we can pick and choose from among the zillions of gadgets those we'd like. We do not see at all that technology has created a new culture. But, counsels William Irwin Thompson in *Evil and World Order:*

> . . . technology is not a tool, it is a culture. As an environment of symbols whose most important expressions are not machines and buildings but the institutions they embody, technology is powerful enough to warp even starlight as it passes through its field. When you live in such an environment, you are not free to pick up one tiny tool and use it as you choose. You are overwhelmingly constrained to perform according to the culture of rationalization and the process definition of values. Because the technocrat claims that values are not eternal *a priori* forms of human consciousness, he is free to bend them to fit the requirements of *his* time.[2]

The culture dimension of technology is easier to see in retrospect. We readily acknowledge that, of course, technology has freed mankind from the limits of the agrarian society. Those were closed societies. Once you lived in one there was no escape.

When a United Nations team asked some Middle East shepherds whether they enjoyed their work, or if they had ever considered doing something else, the shepherds found it impossible even to comprehend the question. Their fathers before them had been shepherds from time immemorial. Their identity was "locked in" to a static conformity. They had no alternative.

Technology brought escape to nearly every major population area of the world. Once freed from the exclusive attention to daily survival, and freed from conformity to a single inherited identity, totally new thinking and doing were possible.

For the first time since the dawn of man we can now see that ordinary people can be emancipated from poverty, from bondage to the soil, from political impotence, from ignorance, and from social discrimination. This is what is meant by the term "quality of possibility." It goes hand in hand with the "level of responsibility."

Western Civilization

The cradle (and the nursemaid) of this extraordinary revolution was Christian Western civilization. The modern technological explosion, says noted historian van Leeuwan:

> . . . is the outcome of a unique course of civilization in the West, in which clearly discernible spiritual motives and a particular view of God, man and the world have played a decisive part.

> . . . looks as though we do indeed stand at the end of an era—an era which started with the Neolithic revolution. Then the foundation was laid for the rise of various civilizations in various regions. Now it is the technological revolution—accomplished by one particular civilization, namely, that of the West—which promises to assume a world-wide character.

> All mankind, whether living at the most primitive level or in the centres of modern civilization, is faced with a process which nothing can either reverse or hold in check—a process of transformation and of the interpenetration of cultures, propelled by the sheer force and forward thrust of the technological revolution.[3]

How did all this come about? William Kuhn, in *Environmental Man,* talks about four periods or groupings that divide man's fundamental response to his surroundings. Each of the four suggests a distinct awareness of the environment, and each, in turn, has affected man himself.[4]

In the first period, primeval man was subordinated to the natural. Nature held the mystery and power of God. Man's response was to try to make life reflect the environment. Rituals and myths were his attempt to participate in the processes of nature, and this is what enriched him spiritually and physically.

The second period is associated with the early civilizations of Babylon, Egypt, and Rome. This was a time when man attempted to disengage himself from his natural environment. He did this by emphasis upon man, rather than man in this world. Man was distinct from his environment. Consequently, this was an anthropomorphic period. It was a period of law, morality, and new cultures that were man-centered.

The third period probably began in the tenth and eleventh centuries. Medieval man began to generalize the concept of mechanical power. The earth was seen as a huge reservoir of energy to be tapped and used according to human intentions. The world could be made to work for man. This era lasted right up into the twentieth century.

The fourth period is one in which man has begun to realize that he can do more than control his environment; he can create it. It is a time when man is more aware of his environment than he has been since primeval days.

Primeval man ritualized his environment, the Graeco-Romans ignored it and thought only about man, and Medieval man began to manipulate and use it. Today, post-modern man creates environments.

Marshall McLuhan reminds us that in the days of the hunter, Paleolithic man was firmly convinced he made his world. He did this by rituals, dances, and various cosmic communing and behavioral patterns. Primitive men, McLuhan says, always thought they made the world. They believed they "wound it up" and renewed its energies by their rituals. Now, asserts McLuhan, man once more "makes" his world. But this time, via technology, we really do.

In part because the shift in perspective is so radical, we are slow to understand that technology is the major force generating our present environment. We err if we simply regard technology as a new form of nature or as a given.

On the other hand, our woes with materialism and the dangers of pollution and nuclear holocaust should not obscure how much good and how much potential for human growth there is in technology. We must be careful, as we alert ourselves to the evils of unbridled technology, not to paint technology with a black brush. The past several centuries have occasioned the rapid unwinding of the bonds of enslavement to forces that allowed but a fraction of human genius to flower. Much of the world population has been set free from a terrible prison and is exploring the land of creativity, involvement, and service. To the extent that technology has released humanity from preoccupation with survival and opened the way to the fullness of life, we can rightfully say that technology has been an instrument of God's grace.

Good and Evil Potentials

The paradox extends also to the potential for good and evil of our liberated civilizations. For it is now feasible to impact via satellite communications or nuclear weaponry the lives of the entire world population.

The present trend towards global unification by means of modern technology is incomparably more intensive

> than anything to which the Roman Empire under Augustus could possibly have aspired.
>
> . . . .
>
> The dimensions of our planetary world bring us into infinitely closer vicinity to the global perspective of the Gospel-proclamation "to all the nations," and likewise to that world-wide power which Satan proposed giving to Jesus. . . .[5]

No wonder we are sometimes numb as we ponder the future. We may feel as Sir Isaac Newton once did, like a child at the seashore "diverting myself in now and then finding a smoother pebble or a prettier shell than ordinary, while the great ocean of truth lay all undiscovered before me."

One temptation is to try to draw the curtain on this intruding reality, to curse technology, and wish for the simpler days of earlier generations. But that is absurd; it is giving the future to those who opt out of being a part of the ongoing process of creation. Another mistake is to automatically associate power with evil, to find danger in new knowledge. Again, that is to remove one's hands from the rudder of life. We must not be afraid to own up to what we have created, for in taking responsibility we are affirming our very humanity.

We must not accede to the cult of valuelessness, meaninglessness, purposelessness. I am convinced that if we are to make it through the tunnel of the present we must marshal, from every quarter, all the forces of health and sanity and purpose we can summon. No segment of our society has a corner on widom, virtue, or understanding about these ultimate questions. But neither can any of us afford to stand aside from the struggle to make the talk of choices into the real stuff of shared life experiences.

How is it some people put it? "Oh, that technology baloney, that future talk, is way over my head. I don't want

to hear about it." Admittedly, life is no longer simple and
it is harder and harder for the ordinary person to understand it. But we must try. Not everyone needs to understand quantum physics; we don't have to be Einsteins to
get a good handle on the world. Understanding begins
with some information. Given a few simple facts, nearly
anyone can comprehend the dangers of air pollution. One
does not need a college education to predict the effects
of a newly automated creamery in a small Midwestern town.
And advanced math is not required to see who will have
to move when an urban renewal project is authorized. The
answers are obvious. But the answers will not come without involved concern. Effort is the cost of understanding.

A Call from Outside

The possibilities in my life and in yours are not fixed
by what we suppose our abilities to be, nor by what others
suppose our abilities are. What I can do and what I must
do are determined by a call that comes to me from outside
myself. In other words, we should not assess our abilities
and inclinations and ask, "What am I suited to do for
God?" No, God comes to each one with a demand that
requires a response: "Here is a job to be done."

Therefore, my aim as a Christian steward of my abilities
must be to break through the limitations of my own stereo-
typed view of myself and put my life into God's frame of
reference. No matter what my abilities, qualifications, or
accomplishments, or lack thereof, when I stand before God
I am naked. "God does not measure the dimensions of a
man by his abilities, his successes, his money, or his talent,
but the fullness of his vision of what God would have him
do and be."

I am a Christian steward of my responses to new opportunities; therefore I will let God seek divine possibilities
in my human activities, both conscious and unconscious.

I will try to be sensitive to what God is calling me to say and do among my fellows. I want to participate in the fullness in small and unplanned ways.

The old debate—"Can man conquer nature with technology?" or "Will technology rule man?"—is no longer relevant. The issue is not either/or. It is not a matter of one subjugating the other. The relevant question for our time is, "What must I learn in order to properly utilize technology as a carefully chosen partner in living?" Technology is neither a savior nor a devil; technology is human consciousness harnessed and unharnessed, concrete and abstract, inert and kinetic. How must we react to it? We must listen to it, assess it, guide it.

Each time scientific knowledge is expanded into new fields or places, we are nudged a little closer to seeing ourselves as belonging to the sequence of creativity and yet standing above it. This duality ensures that the control of the future, which at one time was thought to be determined through the inexorable fulfillment of the laws of nature, is connected through us—to God. We are beginning to see that this world is no longer a place under the sun in which to frolic, unthinking, but that it is a world in which man himself participates as a responsible (able to respond to the Creator) child of God.

The Human and Personal

As Christians become attuned to the challenge that resides in this new understanding of the world, we can begin to move ahead in our acceptance of the new role we must assume. Our task is to bring to every situation the *human,* as distinct from merely the technological; to place the emphasis upon the *personal* over and above the impersonal; to show *wisdom and love* in lieu of spontaneous irresponsibility; to enable both humankind and institutions to see life in its *wholeness,* with *stability* and *purpose.*

The Big World does not live in the stars, space stations,

or electrons. It must come down from the stars and out of the electrons into the hearts of humankind, into our hands and our heads until we have all the boldness that a life can hold.

We must be willing to deal creatively with the most gigantic challenge facing modern man: "How can I work through, and in, the complex techno-social structures, so that these structures might be made to fully serve man in his need? How can I in my own personal role as servant-steward impact the myriad of systems, networks of institutions, channels of communication, and uncounted interactions in our complex world, so that people's lives are enriched?"

The Church's Resources

At this point we might ask, "What are the resources in the Church?" What can the Church do to help in understanding and controlling technology? Christians differ widely in response to these questions, but there is some agreement that the "church faces the task of rethinking her missionary obligation through her encounter with the dangers and expectations of the time." It is essential that first of all the Church "get clear in her own mind what it means, fundamentally, to be living in the technocratic era." [6]

The proper view of this era, insists van Leeuwan, begins with the idea that:

> The Gospel is neither "secular" nor "religious," but it declares the fullness of time to be within human history and is therefore as an eschatological message essentially historical too. The technological revolution is the evident and inescapable form in which the whole world is now confronted with the most recent phase of Christian history. In and through this form Christian history becomes world history. The technocratic era, though it is not the Kingdom of God, is not the kingdom of Satan

either; it is a phase of history in which the Lord and Satan are both at work.[7]

The Church cannot disassociate itself from technology, nor should it expect that with a bit more Christian zeal this new revolution could be a vehicle for returning to a religious world:

> One thing is certain: in no circumstances whatever could this new revolution mean returning to the age of "religion"—and that applies as much to Christianity as to the other religions. We must rid ourselves once and for all of the idea that somehow or other Western civilization has got to be or can be re-Christianized through some restoration, in a new guise, of the *Corpus Christianum.* That civilization today is not less Christian than it was in the Middle Ages; it simply represents a new phase of Christian history.[8]

We are called as a body of Christians to bravely enter the forefront of life to:

> . . . stand and "interpret," until this invading history is no longer suffered as a blind process, a glorious or a pernicious fatality, but men come at last to understand what the voices which speak to them through that history are saying and they learn to distinguish between the voice of Christ and those of his counterfeits.[9]

The Christian claims to have knowledge of God. He claims to point to a convictor that determines his life. He claims that what he does, he does "on purpose." He claims his intellect has been persuaded. He claims his will has been motivated, his desires redirected. In short, he claims he has a purpose. This, surely, is what the world is looking for.

It is very possible that many who do not yet involve themselves in the institutional church have much to contribute. These are people from wide and diverse backgrounds who have a genuine vision for the future. They somehow sense the "theonetic* transition" through which the world is passing. Even so, they are willing to devote their lives, where they are, to the successful fulfillment of this transition into tomorrow. They have accepted the fact that man is born to undertake tasks that never end; that this is part of his humanness. They have been permanently cured of the sickness of a dead end. They are free from the archaic cyclic view of history.

As a result, these men and women are free to be open to one another. They are free to overlook foolish boundaries. They are free to reorient their lives to the shape of things to come. They are free to hold fruitful dialogue with the change-makers who shape tomorrow. They are free from the bondage and stagnation of provincialism. To them this is an age of honesty. No need to fool themselves by turning eyes and ears away from the realities of now.

To be sure, we are all called to deal forthrightly with the future, expressing our faith and hope through involvement and commitment. It is becoming abundantly clear that it is God's will that humanity can and should increasingly consolidate its *responsible* control over creation (Genesis); but more, that "saved" men and women are to work together with all men to establish a political, social, and economic order which will serve humanity (John 13:8) and thereby help individuals, as well as groups, affirm and develop the dignity that is rightfully theirs as children of God.

Our Role as Stewards

Everywhere we turn is a new opportunity to exercise our role as stewards over creation. Stewardship is in the

---

* Theonetics: A new word I coined in 1965 to give a more dynamic quality to the work of God. It means "The study of God in change."

little things, the daily, the immediate; and it is the global: what is good for humankind? mining the ocean, exploring the planets, weather management, nuclear power plants?

Perhaps as we better grasp our potential for participating in creation, we will acquire a new humility and expanded sense of freedom appropriate to our calling.

Just how should we view our humanity? I am not hinting in the slightest that man is God. And yet it is apparent to all that somehow man is being permitted to have more and more dominion over nature, and to understand more fully the *cosmos*. This could lead to prideful self-satisfaction; it could also lead to a higher sense of responsibility. Pascal states it beautifully:

> It is dangerous to show man too clearly how much he resembles the animal, unless we show him his greatness at the same time. But it is also dangerous to show him his greatness, without showing him his baseness. The greatest danger is to leave him in ignorance about one or the other. However, it is most useful to show him both. Man should not believe that he is like an animal, and he should not believe either that he is like an angel. But he should not remain ignorant about one and the other. He must rather know both. Man is not an angel, and not an animal. It is a misfortune that whoever plays the part of an angel will become an animal.

This thing we label humanity is both animal and angel, and *knowing* both. And in so knowing rests the eternal burr in our consciousness. "Man's anxiety is a function of his sheer ambiguity and of his complete powerlessness to overcome that ambiguity, to be straightforwardly an animal or an angel," writes Ernest Becker. "He cannot live heedless of his fate, nor can he take sure control over that fate and triumph over it by being outside the human condition." [10]

There will be a new role for humility in the next century.

Pascal's model is helpful as we exert more and more power over our global future.

One of the by-products of our expanded awareness and power to shape the future is a redefinition of what freedom means. We are in touch with a whole new level and quality of possibility. "New occasions teach new duties," goes the old poem. Freedom in the past meant freedom *from:* from the elements, wild animals, disease, and so forth. Now we must speak of freedom *to:* freedom to be, to do, to utilize our newfound capability. In Christ, God's command becomes, "Live! Be what you are. Let what you are come out. You are free to experience God working through you."

Liberation from Tyranny

Liberty in a Christian is liberation from the tyranny of self-centeredness. It happens in those moments when we step outside the confining framework of routine self-concern. Freedom presupposes the capacity for sacrifice and openness to the living Spirit of God. In other words, we must each become responsive before we can become responsible.

Humble and free, we are peasants on Island Earth. In this last segment of the twentieth century, we are helping to close an era of mankind at least 5,000 years in length. *But we have never managed an entire planet before.* Still, always in the past whenever we faced an uncertain future we never hesitated long—we proceeded. For by some means we held on to a hope, a hope that led us to believe that somehow in the pain and mystery the purposes of God would be revealed. So we went forth, aware, conscious, responsible, trying to become more human by sharing life's hopes, goals, and capabilities with all who live with us on Island Earth.

An authentic individual is neither an end nor a beginning, but a link between ages. Both memory and expectation. Every moment is a new beginning within the continuum of history. It is fallacious to ever segregate a moment and not to sense its involvement in both the past and the future. Humbly the past defers to the future, but refuses to be discarded. Only he who is an heir is qualified to be a pioneer.[1]

Abraham Heschel

Moment by moment the new world arrives. Anxiously we search about for those new men who can guide us into and through the coming world. Deeply we feel the urge to grow and evolve with those men who bring with them the world of human desire. Daringly we venture out to explore our own potential for being such a man. Daily we wrestle with the question: who is the Homonovus? Who is the New Man?[2]

Fred and Anne Cohen Richards

11
Who Is the "New Man"?

Once we have cleared the Herculean hurdle—the mistaken image of human nature as fixed, unchanging and mechanical—we are ready to consider exactly where we stand and where we are going. We can ask with the philosopher, "Where is man?" and apply the energy of the magnetic image of our becoming to the building of a chosen tomorrow.

An Uneasy Adolescence

We may well be tempted to conclude, optimistically, that humanity finally has come of age. But that would place us on the other side of a wide, wide sea that we are just now trying to cross. Rather, with Kenneth Cauthen, I would argue that we are *not yet* adults who have fully "moved out of the innocence, ignorance, and ineptitude of childhood . . . it is much more to the point to see the human race in a stage of uneasy adolescence." [3] Why compare our status now to adolescence? Says Cauthen, we are:

> . . . like a gangly teenager who has begun to taste the joys and sorrows, the responsibilities and dangers, of maturity. Now he clutches pathetically to the fading securities of childhood, hoping with eyes closed for the best; then he rushes blithely ahead, fully confident of his inevitable triumph. Having the burgeoning powers of manhood but little experience of what it means to be a man, his behavior ranges in crazy mixed-up ways from the most irrational stupidity to brilliant sublimity. But within

a few decades the outcome of this adolescent groping
toward adulthood may have largely been decided.[4]

Just as adolescence is a time of emerging new feelings
and capabilities—physical, emotional, intellectual, spiritual—so we are in the midst of a time of what Teilhard
de Chardin describes as the "coming awakeness" of man.
And, writing in *The Future of Man,* he too sees the coming
time as an "apogee" of responsibility and freedom when
we will make a final choice "between arrogant autonomy
and loving excentration." [5]

Being Transformed

By design or accident, consciously or unconsciously, we
are being transformed. Our real education for life is not
in the books or lectures or even the words of television
commentators and personalities; rather it is in the mystique
of the hot knife of technology as it slices through flesh
and blood, and the blunt hammering of personal and impersonal traumatic events on the fragile human spirit.
Lewis Mumford writes about the basis upon which humanity exercises its unique creativity.

> Man's humanity is itself a special kind of efflorescence
> brought about by the favorable conditions under which
> countless other organisms have taken form and repro-
> duced. Over six hundred thousand species of plants,
> over twelve hundred thousand species of animals, helped
> to compose the environment that man found at his dis-
> posal, to say nothing of countless varieties of other or-
> ganisms; some two million species altogether. As human
> populations increased and became regionally differenti-
> ated and culturally identifiable they in turn introduced
> further variety. The maintenance of that variety has been
> one of the conditions of human prosperity; and though
> much of it is superfluous for man's mere survival, *that
> very superfluity has been an incentive for his questing mind.*

[Italics EBL] . . . for the capacity to take in and make
further use of nature's inexhaustible creativity is one
of the underlying conditions for human development.[6]

From Thing to Person

Even though it is difficult to know the extent to which
we have already changed, we can judge according to a
variety of indices that we are moving into a new time.
Our images are changing by degrees. Formerly we were
fully at home with what might be called the "industrial
model" of life—where human activity was centered in digging up and cutting down earth's resources so we could
shape them into millions of products to buy and sell and
consume. But that model has at least been tarnished in
the light of disappearing supplies and escalating rates of
consumption which cannot possibly be sustained for long.
And a new model has moved into the wings. This is the
"relational model" which emphasizes empathy, compassion, trust, nonexploitation, self-esteem, tolerance of ambiguity, humility, patience, and love. Life's essence is person-
to-person rather than person-to-thing.

While the preoccupation with the "sorry mess" or the
"bright promise" of the human condition might seem
merely to be opposite points of view, we find in the heightened interest in self from all sectors one more indication
that humanity is being transformed. When we finally had
enough to eat, when shelter was no longer "if" but "what
part of town you prefer to live in," and when health was
presumed, we turned to things—believing that at last here
was perfect happiness, absolute meaning. But it was a dry
well for the human spirit. Surrounded by things, we could
not shake the haunting questions. We were left with self.
Humanity is capable, seemingly, of anything—even walking
on the moon—but where is meaning and what is happiness? The new craving is to conquer the human problem.

Common Complaints

Accordingly, we survey the obstacles and list them. Some of the more common complaints:

- People don't trust each other anymore. People say one thing and do another.
- Everyone looks out only for himself or herself.
- People just can't agree on anything.
- Most folks feel cut off, disconnected from their past; we are rootless.
- Institutions are cold and uncaring; antiquated rules and needless paperwork get in the way of their real purposes.
- People don't take responsibility for their own lives; everybody wants somebody else to solve the problem but doesn't want to pay for that "luxury."
- Nobody listens to the little guy. If you don't have money or friends in high places you can't change anything.
- The family is doomed; the old values have been lost.

On and on the list goes. We complain in terms of absolutes when we should hedge our frustration and anger with qualifiers such as "seems to." But, of course, we overdraw the picture for emphasis. The danger is not that we are in touch with the negative, but that we give it so much more power than it actually has by virtue of preoccupation, exaggeration, or overstatement.

Paradoxes

In our self-examination, we are helped by stating negatives in the context of positives. We can find a handle on those tricky things *when we approach them as paradoxes.* Increasingly, we see our universe in terms of such paradoxes as these:

People are hungry for fellowship, but are afraid to take the first step of friendship.

We have to look out for our own individual welfare if we are going to be healthy enough to help others.

Everybody is unique, different from everybody else, but we're basically all the same.

People generally share the same basic goals, even though we never stop arguing about what we aspire to.

We want the impossible, but haven't the foggiest notion on how to attain it.

We have to pool our efforts in order to live, but we don't know how to decide who does the "unpleasant" work.

Being dependent upon others frees us to do many things we cannot do when we are trying to be independent.

The more you know, the more you realize how much you don't know.

People need to be with other people and we need to be alone; we require connectedness and isolation.

We both hate and thrive on tension; too much of it and we freeze up, too little and we grow lazy and complacent.

The fun of life is more in the trying to achieve than in reaching the goal.

We learn more from failures than from successes, but energy for bouncing back from failure flows out of the memory of past successes and the dreams of future ones.

Today is a really exciting and challenging time to be alive, if you can stand the pain.

The folk wisdom of the day is rife with these paradoxes, a sure sign of our growing interest in unraveling these "human mysteries." Expanded awareness also extends into the spiritual sphere, where we are expressing a faith-full consciousness that links together some of the apparent (when viewed with old glasses) opposites:

God and man (sharing in the creation process)
The church *in* the world and going unto *all* nations
Faith and works (faith precedes and tempers works)
Worship and work (through worship, work is put in perspective, ordered, and made fruitful)

What is most important in these perceptions is that we are adding reality to the new nature of humankind that we have felt, but did not have words to describe. To paraphrase Goethe, our awareness has been at sea and these thoughts, these paradoxes, have provided a raft.

We should not be alarmed that some ideas lead nowhere, for "the truth of a theory about man is either creative or irrelevant, but never merely descriptive. A theory about the stars never becomes a part of the being of the stars. A theory about man enters his consciousness, determines his self-understanding, and modifies his very existence. The image of man affects the nature of man." [7]

A New Phase

In short, because the image of humankind has taken a quantum leap in breadth and depth in the past few decades, we have approached the end of one phase of human history and tentatively moved into an entirely new phase. I have suggested some of the images that describe this time of transition: The "time between," "adolescence," "the moment after the lightning and before the thunder." Since the image we have of the future is a magnet pulling us out of the present, we should encourage each other in "designing" our new nature.

Probably one of the most thoughtful and exhaustive treatments of the nature of the persons we are becoming is *Homonovus: The New Man* by Fred and Anne Cohen Richards. The picture is drawn of a person who bridges the "chasm between our vision of a new man and a new earth and the daily, concrete realities of modern life" and who "integrates and transforms within himself the heights and depths of human experience. . . ." But most importantly, he "artistically shapes and directs" the contradictions and tensions of our time "toward the creation of the new man and the new earth." [8]

New Man's Nature

New Man is a doer. The magic word is involvement. He is not merely intellectually mulling over a problem; he is committing energy to a "kind of thinking in which ideas, ideals, goals, are existential, efficacious, operationally powerful in leading to decisive change in behavior." [9]

The difference, seemingly small, is effectively illustrated this way:

> Imagine a man high on a cliff overlooking a river. Far below he sees another man in a boat. Suddenly the boat overturns, and the occupant is thrown into the water. Too far away to be of any assistance, the man on the cliff speculates about the options available to the threatened man in the water. Should he try to make it to shore? Would it be better to swim for an island in the middle of the stream? Does his life depend on hanging onto the boat, even though there are dangerous rocks and rapids not far downstream? To the man perched safely above it all, these ideas are idle speculation. He is not threatened; he is not involved. But suppose we switch now to the man thrashing about in the water down below. He too reviews the options, taking into account the relative dangers and prospects each choice offers. But there is a difference in the ideas he runs through his mind. His thinking is existential. He longs for a vision of a real possibility which acted upon effectively will save him. His life is at stake. In his case, insight will lead to action. He can be motivated by a goal that offers him safety.[10]

The point of this illustration is that ideas have powerful consequences only as they are related to a crucial interest. New Man is not merely up on a cliff viewing danger far below and pondering with detachment the many alternatives. New Man is actually in the water; it is his future—personal and corporate—and he has taken it into his own hands.

Secondly, New Man is a risk-taker. He "ventures out to affirm what he perceives to be the growing edge of what it means to be fully human in the present. Risking the journey, he senses he is also a risk taken by creation in the continual unfolding of what man may become. He accepts the challenge. Willingly, courageously, humbly, he embraces the risk and reaches for his best self, for the fullest and most creative realization of his potential for health." [11]

New Man also has vision. He embodies the fullest sense of maturity—thinking a generation ahead. He reasons and prays in terms of the limitless boundaries of the universe. He enhances the finite vision by pushing it ever outward, seeking to know the vision that is God-sent. "What others see as only a personal or historical breakdown, he sees as a potential breakthrough, the stirring and possible birth of a higher form of man." [12]

The ability to "integrate" is important to New Man. He is both thought and passion. "Having experienced the creative shattering of his own foundations—his own limited and narrow perceptions of reality—he hopes, loves, cares, grows, and lives deeply through times that leave others feeling impotent, hopeless, and trapped." [13] He distills meaning, where others only find confusion, by creatively integrating

. . . those polarities traditionally perceived as mutually exclusive opposites in human experience: subjective-objective, self-society, body-mind, masculine-feminine, thinking-feeling, *ad infinitum*. While celebrating human diversity and perceiving clearly particular aspects of the total field of human experience, he perceives and embraces each as related parts of an organic whole, differentiations emerging out of and rooted in a total, universal ground. The tension of opposites becomes the creative urge toward increased wholeness.[14]

His skill in creatively joining together seemingly disparate elements applies specifically to science and technology and the dimensions of the person.

He seeks an application of science and technology that gives human proportions to the world. He takes maximum advantage of the potential in science and technology to liberate persons to be responsible caretakers of nature and enlightened architects of a world increasingly fit for human beings to live in. He believes the ultimate and only real justification for scientific inquiry and technological progress is an increase in human awareness, the enrichment and extension of the collective perceptual world of humankind. His science is person-centered; it is a continually re-examined and re-evaluated commitment to the understanding and celebration of the whole-person-in-community-with-others.[15]

New Man is a decision-maker. He chooses that which elevates his spirit, declines that which debases. This includes choosing friends, companions and co-workers. "He can, without conflict, confront or remove himself from those who seek to disconfirm and invalidate him." This applies equally to institutions—"He confirms and supports those institutions and relationships which promote the positive, healthy, creative satisfaction of human needs" and "rejects and opposes" those which "brutalize, distort, diminish, and stifle the desire and capacity of himself and others to live fully and well." [16]

Diversity a Stimulus

Diversity, to New Man, is a stimulus rather than a damper. "Reverence for life in its diversity and universality and a belief in the dignity and worth of each and every man is his supreme value and ultimate concern." [17] Because he fully understands his own potential, he values the potential of others. He has enough self-esteem and confidence that he never feels the need to tear down someone else. He is refreshed again and again by an appreciation of people's unique qualities and inspired by revelation of what is shared and held sacred by all. His ways are marked by openness, whimsy, playfulness, and flexibility.

New Man has a sense of transcendence that is operative at two levels—his "identity transcends national, religious, social, racial, and cultural barriers," and his life has a vertical plane: He is willing to grapple with, contemplate, study, pray, or simply be open to the possibility that God is seeking him in Christ; he seeks to know and do the will of God, to merge his own understanding of the continuing revelation of God's creation with the counsel and conscience of the Church. The new world that New Man is building is characterized by a decline in religious belief based on fearfulness and authoritarianism, by increased interdenominationalism and ecumenicism, by new forms of religious expression, and by more attention to the moral and ethical dynamics of decisions at all levels of society.

Skill and Sensitivity

Skill and sensitivity in communicating are vital qualities of the New Man. He approaches people as one who is open, authentic, and self-disclosing. "He increasingly embodies—actualizes, models, objectifies, discloses, incarnates, exemplifies—those perceptions and behaviors which promote the maximum growth and well-being of both the

individual and the coming world community." [18] Having
moved from the "you *or* me" world that thrived on missed
signals, I-win/you-lose messages, and broken promises,
New Man cultivates a "you *and* me" sense of community.
Here everyone is a learner, a partner in growth, linked
together by a common vision, interdependency, affection
and responsible two-way communication. Here there is
commitment to the "re-invention of social institutions and
human relationships" in order to break down barriers of
understanding, promote stewardship of earth's resources,
foster new methods of cooperation, and humanize planet
earth.

New Man has a discerning sense of the future. He has
a nose for the "vaguely sensed and almost unexplored
farther reaches of human potential" and the intuitive skill
of knowing when to act.

> He experiences within himself and others, between
> himself and others, that which stirs and moves to take
> man beyond himself. He senses and seeks the creative
> and concrete expression of human potentials unseen and
> unsensed by others. He is open to the unfolding of those
> deeper levels of human awareness presently repressed
> or denied but stirring to emerge. He is the seer, the
> guru-guide, the forerunner.[19]

He thinks beyond what he already comprehends; he
probes paradoxes with the persistence of one who has
tasted the thrill of breakthroughs. Every moment is an
anticipation, waiting to be received.

Together, in community, New Men agree that they cannot remain in the world without moving forward. They
grow, in part, simply by drawing closer together. They
are seeing more and more clearly that we are, all of
us, participants in a process wherein the rebellious seeds
of our individuality can be united and, indeed, must be

for the continued "unfolding of man's potential for wholeness." [20]

Synergy

Because of the creative dynamics of coming together, the total is always greater than the sum of the parts. That is synergy, and the New World is synergistic. It happens as humankind cooperates with the will of God in the ongoing creation process. It says that nothing is without value, that ultimately nothing is lost. Synergy is the predictable unpredictable, is the creative harmony that is born of dissimilarity and tension. It is aliveness—a flow of energy back and forth in the universe, among men and women, and between God and humankind.

Finally, synergy is for the human spirit like that moment in a spacecraft's flight when it continues its outward trajectory into the vast unknowns of the universe rather than slowing to eventually be recaptured by the unrelenting gravitational pull of earth. New Man chooses to go on out, for he is full of hope.

Freedom is a journey with others and for others towards God's future. Freedom can never be defined once and for all. Freedom defined is freedom no longer, because it always transcends all definitions or concepts. It can be experienced and celebrated only as it breaks into our lives as new awareness of hope in God's future and new confidence in the growing ability to experience and share love with others.[1]

Lenny Russell

Hope alone is to be called "realistic," because it alone takes seriously the possibilities with which all reality is fraught. It does not take things as they happen to stand or to lie, but as progressive, moving things with possibilities of change. Only as long as the world and the people in it are in a fragmented and experimental stage which is not yet resolved, is there any sense in earthly hopes. . . .

Thus hopes and anticipations of the future are not a transfiguring glow superimposed upon a darkened existence, but are realistic ways of perceiving the scope of our real possibilities, and as such they set everything in motion and keep it in a state of change. Hope and the kind of thinking that goes with it consequently cannot submit to the reproach of being utopian, for they do not strive after things that have "no place," but after things that have "no place as yet" *but can acquire one.*[2]

Jurgen Moltmann

I consider that what we suffer at this present time cannot be compared at all with the glory that is going to be revealed to us. All of creation waits with eager longing for God to reveal his sons. For creation was condemned to lose its purpose, not of its own

169

will, but because God willed it to be so. Yet there was the hope that creation itself would one day be set free from its slavery to decay and would share the glorious freedom of the children of God. For we know that up to the present time all of creation groans with pain like the pain of childbirth. But it is not just creation alone which groans; we who have the Spirit as the first of God's gifts also groan within ourselves as we wait for God to make us his sons and set our whole being free. For it was by hope that we were saved; but if we see what we hope for, then it is not really hope. For who hopes for something he sees? But if we hope for what we do not see, we wait for it with patience.

Rom. 8:18–28, TEV

12
Hope as the Future Now

Time and time again in history humankind has stood on the threshold of the uncertain. In the face of fear, the black unknown, even certain death, man has somehow mustered the courage to proceed. Why? Why did not the human need of clinging to the known prevail? What is it about us that propels us into the future when the weight of experience would have us dragged screaming, if at all, into the new day?

Hope Makes All the Difference

That special ingredient that makes all the difference is hope. As basic to human nature as consciousness, hope is the dynamic that links the future with the past and present. Hope differs from expectation, although we confuse the two. Expectation merely looks forward to an end result from a predictable process. Expectation is passive. But hope is active—an act of creation; it is creating in the present tense "the space *now* possible for the thing that we are striving for, so that it may come to fulfillment *then*." [3]

Hope transcends the here and now of expectation, as well as plans which arise when one projects from the givens of today what tomorrow will be. Hope is the conscious act of anticipating a future which "reaches out beyond" facts. It is the God-spark of becoming. We cannot underestimate the importance of the distinction between

> . . . existence planned and achieved in terms that are
> possible here and now, and the main concern of this
> existence and what it really wants to be and intends to
> be. This difference, kept awake and made conscious,
> works like a permanent revolution, a permanent icono-
> clasm. It is the motor, the mainspring, the torture of
> history, for it points out the perennial incompleteness
> of that which has become and that which is becoming
> in the reality desired and sought for in hope.[4]

Planning, of course, is extremely important. While planning may be inspired by hope, hope clearly is much more
fundamental and far-reaching. Hope, says Moltmann, an
eminent authority on the subject, is interpersonal—refer-
ring "much less to that future which is available out of
my own powers than to that future which another man
places at my disposal. In that case, hope is not the disposi-
tion of my future, but the expectation of the future of
the other, based on his promise. So hope refers to the
future of the other or to another future." [5]

Moltmann goes on to explain that this "otherness" dimension of the hoped-for future is especially significant
to us as human beings, because it has to do with the "new."
He says this newness "lies on the border between what
is possible and what is impossible. The new is there when
the impossible becomes possible, when the unthinkable
is thought, when the undiscovered is found and
discovered." [6] Therefore, to refuse to hope is to deny the
future.

These pronouncements about hope might well seem to
be so much abstract pie in the sky by some. And yet it is
clear that hope is most "realistic." According to Moltmann,
hope is much more realistic than either presumption—"a
premature, self-willed anticipation of the fulfillment of
what we hope for of God—or despair": "the premature,

arbitrary anticipation of the non-fulfillment of what we hope for from God." [7] Writes Moltmann:

> Hope alone is to be called "realistic," because it alone takes seriously the possibilities with which all reality is fraught. It does not take things as they happen to stand or lie, but as progressing, moving things with possibilities of change. . . . hopes and anticipation of the future are not a transfiguring glow superimposed upon a darkened existence, *but are realistic ways of perceiving the scope of our real possibilities,* and as such they set everything in motion and keep it in a state of change.[8]

The Origin of Hope

This picture of hope is incomplete unless it is linked directly to a belief in God. Hope is of God. It speaks to the full range of possibilities inherent in Creation. It trusts in the eternal goodness of God and not just the knowledge that God exists. To "believe in God is the same as to believe that, contrary to our realistic assessment of the situation, something new and unexpected will suddenly erupt, thus changing completely the possibilities of human life and fulfillment." [9]

Knowledge of God and hope are closely intertwined. But knowledge, in this case, "does not merely reflect past history—as a mental picture of completed facts of history—but it must be an interested knowledge, a practical knowledge, a knowledge that is upheld by confidence in the promised faithfulness of God." [10] We are reminded of the way in which expanding consciousness, as discussed in chapter 5, triggers ever greater consciousness. Knowledge is more than fact accumulation. This is precisely why a liberal arts education is so valuable; it is not locked "into something that is there but rather produces something which is not yet there. It produces by prospecting. It does not bring to light facts or intentions, but rather sets in motion human action." [11]

> Knowledge of God is then an anticipatory knowledge of the future of God, a knowledge of the faithfulness of God which is upheld by the hopes that are called to life by his promises. Knowledge of God is then a knowledge that draws us onwards—not upwards—into situations that are not yet finalized but still outstanding. It is a knowledge not of the looks of past history, but of the outlooks involved in the past promises and past faithfulness of God. Knowledge of God will then anticipate the promised future of God in constant remembrance of the past emergence of God's election, his covenant, his promises and his faithfulness. It is a knowledge that oversteps our bounds and moves within the horizon of remembrance and expectation opened up by the promise, for to know about God is always at the same time to know ourselves called in history by God.[12]

Our Knowledge of God

Our knowledge of God must be placed in an historical context. Over the centuries our understanding of how God acted in history has changed radically. God, as the hope-image of religious people, was essentially a refuge-figure. God was a final answer to suffering, and what was not understood about nature was attributed to God. Hence, for example, lightning storms were seen as acts of God with interpretative meaning. God was "Wholly Other," a mysterious, majestic unknowable Creator.

But, by the time of the twentieth century, most believers did not view God in terms of lightning storms and the like. Science explains these phenomena. The basis of Christian hope had shifted. The God whom we formerly saw as "Wholly Other" was now manifest as the "Wholly New." Centered in the events of the cross, this expanded vision of God perceives God as the God of our future, as the source of our continuing to be made anew. Creation is incomplete and we are participants in the ongoing process. God, instead of a refuge we turn to in desperation for a modicum of order in a chaotic world, has revealed himself in Jesus Christ as the God of everything new.

"Christian hope has its origin in the event of the resurrection of the crucified Christ," writes Moltmann. "In his resurrection, hope is always kindled anew. In him, the future of righteousness and the passing of evil can be hoped for; in him the future of life and the passing of death can be hoped for; in him, the coming of freedom and the passing of humiliation can be hoped for; in him, the future of men's true humanity and the passing of inhumanity can be hoped for." [13]

The cross revealed, metaphorically, the true nature of evil, the failure of living by the Law, and "the unredeemed condition of the world." In the classical language of the Church, we say that in him (the man, Christ, who lived, died, and rose again) is salvation. *Humanity is possible;* God makes us new.

The heart of the Christ event is that our hopes have been turned "to the future of God. It opens up the horizon of the future of fulfillment, for the individual, for mankind as a whole, and the history of all reality. This message of the future is still a matter of hope and longing. Believers continue to pray each day, 'Thy kingdom come.' We look to the future for the source of power to change things as they are." [14]

Moltmann sees hope resting in the event of the history of Christ as a promise "with time still ahead of it" which "turns the present into a front line for the breaking up of the old and the breaking in of the new." Unlike a prophecy, the promise of the Christ-event "requires hope and a new mode of action." [15]

For Christian faith, the fulfillment of the promise and the realization of the hoped-for *novum* is placed in God's hands. The hoped-for future is not only different because it is new but also because it is God's future. Still, this future does not, on the other hand, lie in the hand of blind fate or whimsical chance but rather in the power of this God who will create it.[16]

The believer, "through the history of Christ and the promises of the gospel," becomes oriented to life as an unfolding of God's history—God revealing his future to mankind.

Christian hope not only waits for its fulfillment as a fact but also searches for this fulfillment in the grasping of that which is historically possible. The prospect of this future coming from God already opens up here and now an open space of change and freedom which must be shaped with responsibility and confidence. Through Christ's resurrection and through hope aroused, the future of God exerts an influence in the present and makes the present historical.[17]

Christ—The Embodiment of Hope

Christ, then, is the symbol and the fact, the example and the inspiration of hope. Christ is past, present and future. Not surprisingly, because hope "can be a passion for what has been made possible" in Christ, hope also "becomes a 'passion for what is impossible' " as Kierkegaard noted.[18]

Hope, of course, does not simply drop from the sky. It grows out of faith and is irrevocably connected to faith. "It is through faith that man finds the path of true life, but it is only hope that keeps him on that path," advises Moltmann. "Faith binds man to Christ. Hope sets this faith open to the comprehensive future of Christ." [19]

The Christian perspective is that of a person who

through faith and hope experiences "God happening." We find God "where we wait upon his promises in hope and transformation." Why is this so special? Because this is "a God who calls into being the things that are not, then the things that are not yet, that are the future, also become 'thinkable' because they can be hoped for." [20]

We all know this without knowing *how* it happens. Neither the gospel nor the Christian experience explains the "miracle" of how faith and hope call forth "the future of God." Says Alves, "In traditional theological language, we are not saved by works; *we cannot produce the creative event. We are saved by grace.* The creative event simply takes place and offers itself to us without our being able to provide an explanation for its genesis. The only thing that we can do is *to join it.*" [21]

Anguish and Hope

Those who are convicted in Christ do not necessarily realize the fulfillment of hope on a day-to-day basis. In fact, what often happens is that against the rosy anticipation of the future is the dark cloud of "suffering and the dissatisfaction with the present in which man cannot become man as he hopes." [22] The resulting anguish, more for the whole human condition and especially inequities of suffering and injustice, is not easily stilled. In fact, through the centuries Christian believers, responding to such anguish, have been at the forefront of evolving and revolutionary social change. They have preached a message that stirs the imagination, arouses expectations, and stimulates crusading zeal.

However, no hope-filled Christian can ever actually "reconcile himself with the laws and constraints of this earth, neither with the inevitability of death nor with the evil that constantly bears further evil." [23] Faith, when linked with hope, says Moltmann,

. . . causes not rest but unrest, not patience but impatience. It does not calm the unquiet heart, but is itself this unquiet heart in man. Those who hope in Christ can no longer put up with reality as it is, but begin to suffer under it, to contradict it. Peace with God means conflict with the world, for the goad of the promised future stabs inexorably into the flesh of every unfulfilled present. If we had before our eyes only what we see, then we should cheerfully or reluctantly reconcile ourselves with things as they happen to be. That we do not reconcile ourselves, that there is no pleasant harmony between us and reality, is due to our unquenchable hope. This hope keeps man unreconciled, until the great day of the fulfillment of all the promises of God. It keeps him *in statu viatoris,* in that unresolved openness to world questions which has its origin in the promise of God in the resurrection of Christ and can therefore be resolved only when the same God fulfills his promise. This hope makes the Christian Church a constant disturbance in human society, seeking as the latter does to stabilize itself into a "continuing city." It makes the Church the source of continual new impulses towards the realization of righteousness, freedom and humanity here in the light of the promised future that is to come. This Church is committed to "answer for the hope" that is in it (I Peter 3:15). It is called in question "on account of the hope and resurrection of the dead" (Acts 23:6). Wherever that happens, Christianity embraces its true nature and becomes a witness of the future of Christ.[24]

Braaten, too, describes the Christian revolutionary—someone who is accustomed to thinking in the future tense—as "free both from the terrors of the future and from the tyranny of the past." Unlike other revolutionaries, he does not overexaggerate his self-importance. He "is pulled forward by the vision of the coming kingdom of God" and yet does not allow himself to be "pushed headlong into the future by the trends of the past." He goes against the grain, believing that "a qualitatively different future can be created, actually reversing the trends of the times." [25]

Hope and the Future

This new understanding of Christian hope and the future, particularly their interrelationship, will have a growing impact upon futures thinking and planning. When Christian and futurist are one and the same, two of the four classical ways of thinking and feeling about life and time are linked together. The types, as described by Toynbee, are: (1) Archaism, which dreams of the restoration of an earlier Golden Age; (2) Escapism, which turns away and detaches itself from the world; (3) Futurism, which probes the darkness of an unknown future, and (4) Transfiguration, the Christian belief in the rebirth of this world.

It is impossible to plan without goals, without a vision of the future. Planning, cautions Moltmann, "must be aware of its origin in hope and of the projection of hope. If it puts itself in place of hope, it loses the transcendent impetus of hope and finally also loses itself." [26] The believer knows that in Christ the future of our true humanity can be hoped for, and while planning cannot "make it happen," it does focus energy on what ought to be.

An Act of Love

One of the paradoxes of hope is that it does not convert to dogmatism. Rather, it yields love. *To think in the future tense is an act of love,* for it "looks to the as yet unrealized possibilities of the other, and . . . grants him freedom and allows him a future in recognition of his possibilities." [27] The very nature of this "hope in God's future" precludes self-redemption through any real or imagined "good works," and so the way is "open for loving, ministering self-expenditure in the interests of a humanizing of conditions and in the interests of the realization of justice in the light of the coming justice of God." [28]

The proper view of the world, says Moltmann, is that it is

> . . . engaged in a history. It is therefore the world of possibilities, the world in which we can serve the future, promised truth and righteousness and peace. This is an age of diaspora, of sowing in hope, of self-surrender and sacrifice, for it is an age which stands within the horizon of a new future. Thus self-expenditure in this world, day-to-day love in hope, becomes possible and becomes human within that horizon of expectation which transcends this world.[29]

In Christ we have been given the gift of commitment to the future; the power of God is in our midst. And we are free to stand before eternal possibilities, to transcend the present. In Christ the promises of God—the future of God—are confirmed and validated *but not yet completely fulfilled.*

For me to think in the future tense is to join in God's great and good Creation, seeing in hope an affirmation of the importance of my participation, my love. As we each ponder our roles in building tomorrow, we might borrow a leaf from a member of the Connecticut Assembly in 1780 who . . .

> . . . when proceedings were threatened by panic induced by a darkening of the sky so unprecedented as to suggest the arrival of a prophesied Judgment Day. He ruled—"Either this is the end of the world or it is not. If it is not, our business should proceed. If it is, I prefer to be found doing my duty. Let lights be brought."

Let lights be brought. Not more power; but that much rarer, subtler, more demanding fruit of the human spirit—more light.

Notes

Chapter 1

1. Malachi Martin, *The New Castle* (New York: E. P. Dutton & Company, Inc., 1974), pp. 4–5.
2. Gerald and Patricia Mische, *Toward a Human World Order* (New York: Paulist Press, 1977), p. 352.
3. John McHale, *The Future of the Future* (New York: Ballantine Books, Inc., 1971), p. 65.
4. José Ortega y Gasset, *Man and Crisis* (New York: W. W. Norton & Co., Inc., 1958), p. 109.
5. *Ibid.,* p. 120.
6. *Ibid.,* p. 203.
7. Geoffrey Vickers, *Freedom in a Rocking Boat* (Allen Lane: The Penguin Press, 1970), p. 15. Copyright © Geoffrey Vickers, 1970.
8. Mische, *op. cit.,* p. 352.

Chapter 2

1. Eric Hoffer, *The Temper of Our Times* (New York: Harper & Row Publishers, Inc., 1967), p. 37.
2. Carl Sagan, *The Dragons of Eden* (New York: Random House, Inc., 1977), p. 236.
3. Allen Wheelis, *How People Change* (New York: Harper & Row Publishers, Inc., 1973).

Chapter 3

1. I. Rice Pereira, *The Transcendental Formal Logic of the Infinite: The Evolution of Cultural Forms* (Published by the author, © 1966), p. 43. Reprinted with permission of the Corcoran Gallery of Art and the I. Rice Pereira Foundation, Washington, D. C.

2. Walter J. Ong, *Knowledge and the Future of Man* (New York: Holt, Rinehart, and Winston, 1968), p. 3.

3. Peter Drucker, *Landmarks of Tomorrow* (New York: Harper & Row Publishers, Inc., 1957), p. 2.

4. *Ibid.*, p. 4.

5. *Ibid.*, p. 5.

6. *Ibid.*, p. 6.

7. *Ibid.*, p. 11.

8. *Ibid.*, pp. 15–16.

9. William Lynch, S. J., *Images of Faith, An Exploration of the Ironic Imagination* (Notre Dame: University of Notre Dame Press, 1973), p. 12.

10. Robert K. Greenleaf, *Jefferson House* (An unpublished manuscript).

Chapter 4

1. Werner Heisenberg, *Physics and Beyond, Encounters in Conversation* (New York: Harper & Row Publishers, Inc., 1971), p. 70.

2. Fritjof Capra, *The Tao of Physics* (Boulder: Shambhala Publications, Inc., 1975), p. 20. (Reprinted by special arrangement with Shambhala Publications, Inc.)

3. *Ibid.*, p. 20.

4. Victor Guillemin, *The History of Quantum Mechanics* (New York: Charles Scribner's Sons, 1968), p. 5.

5. Capra, *op. cit.*, p. 56.

6. *Ibid.*, p. 61.

7. *Ibid.*, p. 62.

8. *Ibid.*, p. 64.

9. Guillemin, *op. cit.*, p. 9.

10. Capra, *op. cit.*, p. 65.

11. *Ibid.*, p. 68.

12. Arthur Koestler, *Roots of Coincidence* (New York: Random House, Inc., 1972), p. 50.

13. Capra, *op. cit.*, p. 80.

14. Harold Schilling, *The New Consciousness in Science and Religion* (New York: United Church Press, 1973), p. 83. Reprinted by permission of The Pilgrim Press from Harold K. Schilling, *The New Consciousness in Science and Religion* (New York: The Pilgrim Press, 1973). Copyright © 1973 United Church Press.

15. Ibid., p. 52.

16. Heisenberg, *op. cit.*, p. 77.

17. Schilling, *op. cit.*, p. 52.

18. *Ibid.*, p. 79.

19. *Ibid.*, p. 76.

20. *Heisenberg*, op. cit., pp. 40–41.

21. *Ibid.*, p. 123.

22. Schilling, *op. cit.*, p. 47.

23. *Ibid.*, p. 89.

Chapter 5

1. T. S. Eliot, "Little Gidding," from *Four Quartets* (New York: Harcourt Brace & World, 1943), p. 31.

2. I. Rice Pereira, *The Nature of Space* (Published by the author, © 1968), pp. 48–50.

3. William Irwin Thompson, *At the Edge of History* (New York: Harper & Row Publishers, Inc., 1971), p. 230.

4. José Ortega y Gasset, *Man and Crisis* (New York: W. W. Norton & Co., Inc., 1958), p. 50.

5. *Ibid.*, p. 50.

6. Marshall McLuhan, *Understanding Media* (Hightstown: McGraw-Hill Book Co., 1964), p. 237.

7. Edward T. Hall, "Proxemics," *Current Anthropology* (April–June, 1968), p. 84.

8. Robert E. Neil, "The Relevant Issue," *Oberlin Alumni Journal* (May, 1969).

9. Victor Ferkiss, *The Future of Technological Civilization* (New York: George Braziller, Inc., 1974), p. 4.

10. Pereira, *The Nature of Space,* pp. 6–7.

11. *Ibid.,* pp. 8–9.

12. *Ibid.,* p. 30.

13. *Ibid.,* p. 34.

14. *Ibid.,* pp. 48–50.

15. *Ibid.,* pp. 54–55.

16. *Ibid.,* p. 60.

17. *Ibid.,* p. 50.

Chapter 6

1. Teilhard de Chardin, *The Future of Man* (New York: Harper & Row Publishers, Inc., 1964), p. 98.

2. Mircea Eliade, *Cosmos and History* (New York: Harper & Row Publishers, Inc., 1959), p. 11.

3. Edward B. Lindaman, *Space: A New Direction for Mankind* (New York: Harper & Row Publishers, Inc., 1969), p. 158.

Chapter 7

1. Mische, *op. cit.,* p. 353.

2. Robert Pirsig, *Zen and the Art of Motorcycle Maintenance* (New York: William Morrow & Company, Inc., 1974), p. 152.

Chapter 8

1. Teilhard de Chardin, *op. cit.,* p. 19.

2. Abraham Heschel, *The Insecurity of Freedom* (New York: Farrar, Straus & Giroux, 1966), p. 158. From *The Insecurity of Freedom* by Abraham Joshua Heschel, Copyright © 1959, 1960, 1963, 1964, 1966 by Abraham Joshua Heschel, Farrar, Straus & Giroux, Inc.

3. Mische, *op. cit.,* p. 351.

4. Erich Fromm, *To Have or to Be* (New York: Harper & Row, Publishers, Inc., 1976), p. 76.

5. Simple Living Collective, *Taking Charge* (New York: American Friends Service Committee, 1977), p. 11. (Reprinted by permission of Bantam Books, Inc.) From *Taking Charge* by the Simple Living Collective Copyright © 1977 by American Friends Service Committee. Reprinted by permission of Bantam Books, Inc.

6. Fromm, *op. cit.*, p. 27.

7. Abraham Heschel, *Who Is Man?* (Stanford: Stanford University Press, 1965), p. 57.

8. Geoffrey Vickers, *op. cit.*, p. 183.

9. *Ibid.*, pp. 183–184.

10. Elton Trueblood, *The Validity of the Christian Mission* (New York: Harper & Row Publishers, Inc., 1972), p. 96.

Chapter 9

1. Loren Eisely, *The Unexpected Universe* (New York: Harcourt, Brace & World, Inc., 1969), p. 7.

2. Barbara Ward, *Spaceship Earth* (New York: Columbia University Press, 1966), p. 111.

3. Heschel, *Who Is Man?*, p. 68.

4. Lewis Mumford, *The Myth of the Machine: Technics and Human Development* (New York: Harcourt, Brace, & Jovanovich, Inc., 1967), p. 9.

5. Heschel, *Who Is Man?*, p. 104.

6. *Ibid.*, p. 68.

7. Ruben Alves, *Tomorrow's Child* (New York: Harper & Row Publishers, Inc., 1972), pp. 198–199.

8. *Ibid.*, p. 199.

9. *Ibid.*, p. 201.

Chapter 10

1. Abraham Heschel, *Man's Quest for God* (New York: Charles Scribner's Sons, 1954), p. xiii.

2. William Irwin Thompson, *Evil and World Order* (New York: Harper & Row Publishers, Inc., 1976), p. 22.

3. Arend T. van Leeuwan, *Christianity and World History* (New York: Charles Scribner's Sons, 1964), p. 401.

4. William Kuhn, *Environmental Man* (New York: Harper & Row Publishers, Inc., 1969), pp. 128–131.

5. van Leeuwan, *op. cit.,* p. 406–407.

6. *Ibid.,* p. 408.

7. *Ibid.*

8. *Ibid.,* p. 410.

9. *Ibid.,* p. 409.

10. Ernest Becker, *Denial of Death* (New York: The Free Press, A Division of The Macmillan Co., 1977), p. 69.

Chapter 11

1. Heschel, *Who Is Man?,* p. 99.

2. Fred and Anne Cohen Richards, *Homonovus* (Boulder, Col.: Shields Publishing Co., Inc., 1972), p. 146.

3. Kenneth Cauthern, *Christian Biopolitics* (Nashville: Abingdon Press, 1971), p. 24. Used by permission.

4. *Ibid.*

5. Teilhard de Chardin, *op. cit.,* p. 19.

6. Mumford, *op. cit.,* p. 37.

7. Heschel, *Who Is Man?,* p. 8.

8. Richards, *op. cit.,* p. 146.

9. Cauthern, *op. cit.,* p. 57.

10. *Ibid.*

11. Richards, *op. cit.,* p. 147.

12. *Ibid.*

13. *Ibid.*

14. *Ibid.,* p. 148.

15. *Ibid.,* p. 150.

16. *Ibid.,* p. 149.

17. *Ibid.,* p. 148.

18. *Ibid.,* p. 147.

19. *Ibid.,* p. 149.

20. *Ibid.,* p. 151.

Chapter 12

1. Lenny Russell, *Human Liberation in a Feminist Perspective* (Philadelphia: The Westminster Press, 1974), p. 25.

2. Jurgen Moltmann, *Theology of Hope* (New York: Harper & Row Publishers, Inc., 1967), p. 25.

3. Alves, *op. cit.,* p. 197.

4. Jurgen Moltmann, *Hope and Planning* (New York: Harper & Row Publishers, Inc., 1971), p. 196.

5. *Ibid.,* pp. 180–181.

6. *Ibid.*

7. Moltmann, *Theology of Hope,* p. 23.

8. *Ibid.,* p. 25.

9. Alves, *op. cit.,* p. 195.

10. Moltmann, *op. cit.,* p. 118.

11. Moltmann, *Hope and Planning,* p. 190.

12. Moltmann, *Theology of Hope,* p. 118.

13. Moltmann, *Hope and Planning,* pp. 194–195.

14. Carl E. Braaten, *The Future of God: The Revolutionary Dynamics of Hope* (New York: Harper & Row Publishers, Inc., 1969), pp. 24–25.

15. Moltmann, *Hope and Planning,* p. 183.

16. *Ibid.*

17. *Ibid.*

18. Moltmann, *Theology of Hope,* p. 20.

19. *Ibid.*

20. *Ibid.,* p. 30.

21. Alves, *op. cit.,* p. 198.

22. Moltmann, *Hope and Planning,* p. 197.

23. Moltmann, *Theology of Hope,* p. 21.

24. *Ibid.,* pp. 21–22.

25. Braaten, *op. cit.,* p. 157.

26. Moltmann, *Hope and Planning,* p. 194.

27. Moltmann, *Theology of Hope,* p. 338.

28. *Ibid.*

29. *Ibid.*

Selected Readings

Barbour, Ian. *Myths, Models, and Paradigms.* New York: Harper & Row Publishers, Inc., 1974.

Bauer, Raymond. *Social Indicators.* Cambridge: M.I.T. Press, 1966.

Becker, Ernest. *Escape from Evil.* New York: The Macmillan Co., 1976.

————. *The Structure of Evil.* New York: George Braziller, Inc., 1968.

Berger, Peter L., and Luckmann, Thomas. *The Social Construction of Reality.* Garden City: Doubleday & Company, Inc., 1966.

Boulding, Kenneth. *The Meaning of the Twentieth Century: The Great Transition.* New York: Harper & Row Publishers, Inc., 1964.

Bundy, Robert. *Images of the Future: The Twenty-first Century and Beyond.* Buffalo, New York: Prometheus, 1976.

Cleveland, Harland. *A Future Executive.* New York: Harper & Row Publishers, Inc., 1972.

Cornish, Edward. *The Study of the Future.* Washington, D. C.: World Future Society, 1977.

DeJouvenal, Bertrand. *The Art of Conjecture.* New York: Basic Books, 1964.

Esfandiary, F. M. *Optimism One.* New York: W. W. Norton & Co., Inc., 1971.

Goodwin, Richard. *The American Condition.* Garden City: Doubleday & Co., Inc., 1974.

Gray, Elizabeth; Gray, David Dodson; and Martin, William F. *Growth and Its Implications for the Future.* Branford, Conn.: The Dinosaur Press, 1975.

Gustavson, Carl G. *A Preface to History.* Hightstown, N.J.: McGraw-Hill Book Co., 1955.

Johnston, William. *Silent Music.* New York: Harper & Row Publishers, Inc., 1974.

Kuhn, Thomas. *The Structure of Scientific Revolutions.* Chicago, Illinois: University of Chicago Press, 1962.

Kung, Hans. *On Being a Christian.* New York: Doubleday & Co., Inc., 1976.

Lodge, George Cabot. *The New American Ideology.* New York: Random House, 1975.

Martin, Gardner. *Relativity for the Millions.* New York: Pocket Books, Inc., 1965.

Maruyama, Magoroh; and Hawkins, Arthur, Eds. *Culture Beyond the Earth: The Role of Anthropology in Outer Space.* New York: Random House, Inc., 1975.

Mazlish, Bruce. *The Railroad and the Space Age, An Exploration in Historical Analogy.* Cambridge, Mass.: M.I.T. Press, 1965.

McHale, John. *World Facts and Trends.* The Macmillan Co., Collier Books, 1972.

Mead, Margaret. *World Enough, Rethinking the Future.* Boston, Mass.: Little, Brown & Co., 1975.

Mesarovic, Mihajlo; and Pestel, Edward. *Mankind at the Turning Point.* New York: Dutton/Readers Digest Press, 1974.

Niebuhr, H. Richard. *The Meaning of Revelation.* New York: The Macmillan Co., 1974.

North, Robert C. *The World that Could Be.* Stanford Alumni Ass'n: The Portable Stanford Series, 1976.

Novak, Michael. *Ascent of the Mountain, Flight of the Dove.* New York: Harper & Row Publishers, Inc., 1971.

Nouwen, Henry J. M. *The Wounded Healer.* Garden City: Doubleday & Co., Inc., 1972.

Polak, Fred. *The Image of the Future.* San Francisco: Jossey-Bass, 1972.

Polanyi, Michael. *The Tacit Dimension.* Garden City: Doubleday & Co., Inc., 1966.

Saroson, Seymour B. *The Creation of Settings and the Future Societies.* San Francisco: Jossey-Bass, 1972.

Schillebeeckx, Edward. *God the Future of Man.* New York: Sheed & Ward, 1968.

Schumacher, E. F. *A Guide for the Perplexed.* New York: Harper & Row Publishers, Inc., 1977.

Schwartz, Tony. *Responsive Chord.* Garden City: Doubleday & Co., Inc., 1972.

Shane, Harold G. *The Educational Significance of the Future.* Bloomington, Indiana: Phi Delta Kappa Educational Foundation, 1973.

Theobald, Robert. *An Alternative Future for America II.* Chicago, Illinois: Swallow Press, 1970.

Toffler, Alvin. *Learning for Tomorrow.* New York: Random House, 1974.

Trueblood, Elton. *The Validity of the Christian Mission.* New York: Harper & Row Publishers, Inc., 1972.

Turnbull, Colin M. *The Mountain People.* New York: Simon & Schuster, Inc., 1973.

Vickers, Geoffrey. *Value Systems and Social Process.* London: Tavistock Publications, 1968.

White, Lynn. *Dynamo and Virgin Reconsidered.* Cambridge, Mass.: M.I.T. Press, 1968.

Willis, Edward David. *Daring Prayer.* Atlanta: John Knox Press, 1977.

World Future Society. *The Future: A Guide to Information Sources.* Washington, D. C.: World Future Society, 1977.